Interlanguage Refusals

Walter de Gruyter · 250 · 1749 · 1999 · Berlin · New York

Studies on Language Acquisition   15

Editor

Peter Jordens

Mouton de Gruyter
Berlin   ·   New York

Susan M. Gass and Noël Houck

Interlanguage Refusals
A Cross-cultural Study of Japanese-English

W DE G

Mouton de Gruyter
Berlin · New York 1999

Mouton de Gruyter (formerly Mouton, The Hague)
is a Division of Walter de Gruyter & Co., Berlin.

The series Studies on Language Acquisition was formerly
published by Foris Publications, Holland.

♾ Printed on acid-free paper which falls within the guidelines of the
ANSI to ensure permanence and durability.

Library of Congress Cataloging-in-Publication Data

Gass, Susan M.
    Interlanguage refusals : a cross-cultural study of Japanese-English /
Susan M. Gass and Noël Houck.
        p.   cm. − (Studies on language acquisition ; 15)
    Includes bibliographical references (p.   ) and indexes.
    ISBN 3-11-016386-1 (alk. paper). − ISBN 3-11-016387-X (pbk. :
alk. paper)
    1. English language − Study and teaching − Japanese speakers.
2. English language − Grammar, Comparative − Japanese.   3. Japanese language − Grammar, Comparative − English.   4. Interlanguage
(Language learning)   5. Intercultural communication.   6. Speech acts
(Linguistics)   I. Houck, Noël, 1942−   II. Title.   III. Series.
PE1130.J3G37   1999
428'.0071−dc21   99-24530
                                                                              CIP

Die Deutsche Bibliothek − Cataloging-in-Publication Data

Gass, Susan M.:
Interlanguage refusals : a cross cultural study of Japanese English / Susan
M. Gass and Noël Houck. − Berlin ; New York : Mouton de Gruyter,
1999
    (Studies on language acquisition ; 15)
    ISBN 3-11-016386-1

Printing: Werner Hildebrand, Berlin.
Binding: Lüderitz & Bauer GmbH, Berlin.
Printed in Germany.

Acknowledgments

This book is the result of work that began in 1989 when we became interested in the pragmatic performance of second language learners. Some of the chapters have appeared in somewhat different versions in other publications. Notably, parts of Chapter Two originally appeared as "Non-native refusals: A methodological perspective," in Gass and Neu (1996), Chapter Four (Houck and Gass 1997) appeared in *Silence: Interdisciplinary Perspectives* (ed. by Adam Jaworski), Chapter Five was published by Noël Houck (1998) in *Proceedings of the 9th Conference on Second Language Research in Japan* (ed. by Fujimura, Kato, and Smith) and parts of Chapter Eight come from Gass (1997). We would like to thank Joyce Neu and Adam Jaworski for helpful comments on these earlier versions. Figure 11 in Chapter 8 is reprinted with permission of Blackwell Publishers Ltd. We are also grateful to Ildikó Svetics of Michigan State University who read through a near final version and provided insightful and detailed comments. Dennie Hoopingarner helped us in innumerable ways with computer problems. Barbara Hird, our indexer, was patient while we put the "finishing touches" on the manuscript. Finally, Katja Huder of Mouton was always prompt in responding to our (at times) petty questions. We appreciate her working through many of the details of publication with us. Although each of these individuals was helpful in different ways, they are in no way responsible for any errors that may remain.

Over the years, our work evolved through conference presentations, published work, and, in general, conversations with colleagues. In this regard we are particularly grateful to Leslie Beebe and Miriam Eisenstein who year after year have tirelessly organized the TESOL Sociolinguistics Colloquium in which much of our work was initially presented. We also recognize the contributions and comments made by many of our colleagues, notably Andrew Cohen and Elite Olshtain, who also regularly presented in that colloquium.

Conducting cross-oceanic collaboration has not been easy. The airlines are, we are sure, grateful to us for our numerous trips back and forth and we are grateful to them for the many frequent flyer miles we have racked up in the preparation of this book.

Finally, our families who have put up with this travel are owed a debt of gratitude — especially for cooking when we could scarcely take time to eat. Thanks Michael for making soup and thanks Josh for baking bagels!

Susan Gass   Noël Houck
Okemos, Michigan   Tokyo, Japan

Contents

Appendices

Chapter 1
The study of refusals

1. Introduction

The study of speech acts provides researchers with a window on human interaction. Blum-Kulka, House, and Kasper (1989) claim that the investigation of speech acts among other things 1) allows researchers to make claims of universality, 2) reveals the social implications conveyed by modes of performance, and 3) uncovers cultural differences in interactive strategies. In the past 15-20 years, there has been significant activity related to the study of speech acts. Studies have been broad in scope, treating speech acts in a variety of languages, cultures, and discourse communities. In general, research has focused on 1) the realization of a particular speech act within a given language, 2) the realization of a particular speech act across languages, or 3) the production (or, occasionally recognition) of a particular speech act in a language by non-native speakers of that language.

Analysis of individual speech acts has frequently been based on a framework of primary features such as alerters, supportive moves, and the head act, along with the upgraders and downgraders that are associated with the utterance used to perform the act (Blum-Kulka, House, and Kasper 1989). In particular, attention has focused on the nature of the head act, the act that conveys the specific illocution under study.

The main approach to analysis has been to categorize the realizations of the speech act under study, usually according to classes of strategies or semantic formula, often with a separate classification of modifiers included. Additionally, many researchers have investigated the effects of various social factors on the formulation of the speech act or the effects of different linguistic realizations (e.g., syntactic form, modifier) on the acceptability of the act.

In analyzing the data to be presented in this book, we too will identify the strategies used to perform a speech act, in this case, the speech act of refusal. However, in addition, we will investigate the behaviors used by non-native speakers as they negotiate their way through a complete refusal interaction. These behaviors take us well beyond the linguistic and propositional characteristics of an individual act and into the area of unfolding sequences. We will consider non-native speakers' verbal and nonverbal behavior; their language and nonverbal actions both when they are the primary speaker and when they are listening. We will then infer how the on-line behaviors manifested by the non-native speakers and their interlocutors may play a role in both the successful performance of a face-threatening act and the acquisition of pragmatic competence.

This book has as its main goal the study and description of refusal sequences as exemplified through the verbal and nonverbal performance of a group of second language speakers — Japanese learners of English. Before detailing the data-base and performing an initial analysis of the data (Chapter Two), we situate the present study within a general framework of refusals and consider analytic schemata used in previous studies of refusals.

2. Refusals

Among those speech acts that have received a great deal of scrutiny are requests, apologies, compliments, and, increasingly, refusals. It is on refusals that this book focuses.

A refusal is generally considered a speech act by which a speaker "denies to engage in an action proposed by the interlocutor" (Chen, Ye, and Zhang 1995: 121). Refusals are one of a relatively small number of speech acts which can be characterized as a response to another's act (e.g., to a request, invitation, offer, suggestion), rather than as an act initiated by the speaker. Because refusals normally function as second pair parts, they preclude extensive planning on the part of the refuser. And because extensive planning is limited, and because the possibilities for a response are broader than for an initiating act, refusals may reveal greater complexity than many other speech acts.

Refusals are often played out in lengthy sequences involving not only negotiation of a satisfactory outcome, but face-saving maneuvers to accommodate the noncompliant nature of the act. Because of the face-threatening nature of refusals, they are often regulated by different cross-cultural face concerns. Consequently, they may be exceptionally subtle. In fact, as Lyuh (1992) notes in work on Korean refusals, "it is sometimes difficult to recognize refusals even in one's native language" (p. 13).

Given the less constrained nature of refusals (when compared to other speech acts), appropriate comprehension and production require a certain amount of often culture-specific knowledge and ability on the part of the refuser. This situation makes accurate information on the characteristics of culturally appropriate refusals of potential interest not only to researchers, but to second and foreign language teachers and students as well.

3. Possible refusal trajectories

As stated above, refusals are acts that function as a response to an Initiating Act. There are a number of possible Initial Responses after an Initiating Act such as a request; similarly, there are a number of possible Final Outcomes. It is important to note that the Initial Response and Final Outcome may not coincide.[1] Table One represents the various possibilities at each stage of a refusal interaction in response to a request, invitation, offer, or suggestion.

The Initiating Act sets the process in motion. Two general types of Initial Response by a Respondent are possible. The Respondent can either accept or not accept. An Accept in this case refers to sincere acceptance, that is, an acceptance that is intended as agreement and is perceived as such. With Nonaccepts, the situation becomes more complex, particularly because numerous options confront a refuser. A Nonaccept can be expressed as a refusal, a postponement, or the proposal of an alternative.

If the response is a Nonaccept, the Initiator can concur or go along with the Respondent's Nonaccept (refusal, postponement, or proposed alternative), in which case the current interaction is resolved, and the Initial Response serves as the Final Outcome.

Table 1. Possible responses and outcomes

Initiating Act (Initiator=I)	Initial Response (Respondent=R)	Response to R's Nonaccept (I)	Final Outcome
Request Invitation Offer Suggestion	Sincere Accept Nonaccept -- Refuse -- Postpone (Sincere) -- Propose Alternative	NA Acceptance of R's Nonaccept Nonacceptance of R's Nonaccept →Negotiation (Abandon Process)	Acceptance Refusal Postponement Compromise (on an Alternative Action/Nonaction)

On the other hand, if the Initiator does not accede to the Respondent's Nonaccept, the Initiator can attempt to work out a more acceptable resolution. This circumstance leads to negotiation, where negotiation is part of an interaction in which the interactants perform a series of linguistic acts with the goal of producing a (perhaps mutually) satisfactory Final Outcome.[2]

Negotiation can involve Initiator recyclings of the Initiating Act, reasons for acceptance, proposals of alternatives, or even suggestions of postponement. It can also involve discussion of any of the above, as well as the Respondent's responses and initiations, and discussion of the Respondent's contributions. What is important about a situation in which the Initiator does not accept the Respondent's Nonaccept is that it usually involves some sort of negotiation, and since negotiation is a recursive phenomenon, various Outcomes can follow on the heels of different Initial Responses (see also Edmondson 1981).

The Final Outcome refers to the resolution of the interaction, the status of the action (or nonaction) by the Respondent that is in force at the end of the interaction. The range of Outcomes is represented in Figure 1.

The Final Outcome can be acceptance (complete or conditional), refusal, postponement, or an alternative action or compromise by the respondent. The existence of a Final Outcome to a particular interaction does not mean that follow-up will not occur at a later time, only that a Final Outcome has been determined for the interaction under consideration.

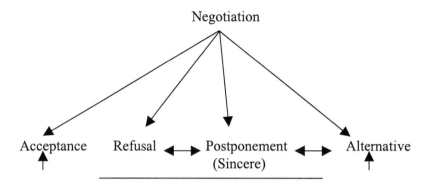

Figure 1. Possible negotiation outcomes

It is also possible that at some point the Initiator will abandon the interaction without coming to any resolution with the Respondent. Although this may be taken as acceptance of whatever response was currently on the table, it need not necessarily be. Thus, if an Initiator does not accept the Respondent's Nonaccept, she or he may either engage in negotiation or abandon the interaction.

The Final Outcome may or may not be mutually satisfactory. Importantly, it must be noted that what constitutes a satisfactory outcome may vary cross-culturally (see Kitao 1997).

Note that this model can be viewed as an elaborated version of what Labov and Fanshel (1977) call a "refusal sequence." Focusing on responses to requests, Labov and Fanshel note that there are three modes of response. First, one can comply either by providing (or agreeing to provide) the requested information or by performing (or agreeing to perform) the requested action, as in the following invented examples.

(1) Compliance with a request (performance of an action)

    John: Would you be able to help me with my homework this evening?

Mary: Sure. Let's take a look at where you're having problems.

(2) Compliance with a request (agreement to perform an action)

John: Would you be able to help me with my homework this evening?
Mary: Sure, I'd be glad to. What time would you like to get together?

Another possible response is to put off the request (see Example 3):

(3) Putting off a request[3]

John: Would you be able to help me with my homework this evening?
Mary: Didn't you tell me you'd already done your homework?

In such instances, the request can be reinstated after the put-off has been dealt with, or it can be withdrawn. The third possible response is to refuse the request with or without an accounting, as in Examples (4) and (5).

(4) Refusal of a request — without accounting

John: Would you be able help me with my homework this evening?
Mary: Sorry, I can't.

(5) Refusal of a request — with accounting

John: Would you be able to help me with my homework this evening?
Mary: Sorry, I can't. I have to work late.

Labov and Fanshel note that there is considerable overlap between their put-offs, which are frequently intended as refusals, and refusals with accountings, both of which may be treated as refusals by the requester. And, in fact, we will be treating put-offs as one type of refusal (see Chapter Two).

Labov and Fanshel make the point that responses that are taken as refusals often result in what might be referred to as recycling. In their words

> Since most refusals involve an accounting in some form, such as a request for further information, they can be defined by the requester as only temporary refusals….Such a situation sets up the possibility of a long chain of repeated requests (p. 93).

The model that we are proposing goes into considerable detail, viewing the rejection of a Nonaccept to an Initiating Act such as a request, invitation, offer, or suggestion as setting up the possibility of negotiation. This negotiation may consist of a long chain of recyclings of the Initiating Act but may also involve more complex interaction. See Figure 2 for an overview of possible refusal trajectories.

4. Categorizing refusal responses

In the model proposed above, the assumption is made that acts such as acceptance, refusal, postponement, and proposal of alternative will be easily identifiable as such by the addressee and by the researcher who observes and codes the response(s). This is not necessarily the case, particularly with refusals. In this section, we discuss difficulties confronted by researchers in identifying refusals, as well as several systems used by researchers to classify refusal strategies.

4.1. *Identifying refusal features*

Clearly, utterances may differ in the explicitness with which a particular act is expressed. The nature or identity of the act may be directly interpretable from the presence of linguistic features such as verb mood (e.g., imperative, interrogative) or a performative verb —

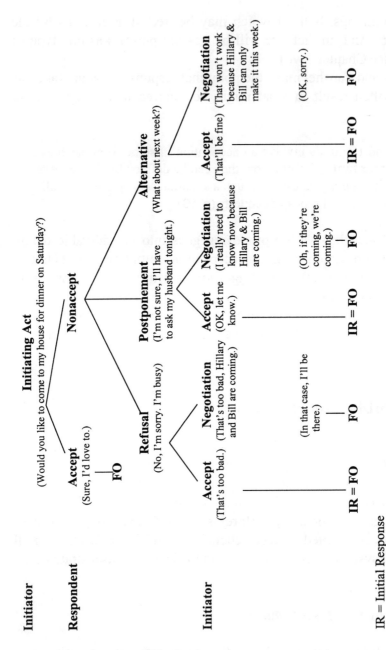

IR = Initial Response
FO = Final Outcome (= Accept, Refusal, Postponement, or Alternative)

Figure 2. Possible refusal trajectories involving negotiation

a verb which names the act that it is performing (e.g., "I apologize," "I promise"). These features are frequently referred to as illocutionary force indicating devices. The nature of an act may also be determined, somewhat less directly, by the semantic content of the utterance. Consider the utterance "I would appreciate it if the window were closed." Even though the linguistic form is a simple informative statement with an if-clause, and the main verb is not a performative verb, the utterance can be interpreted as a request to close the window. This is at least partially a result of the semantic content of the utterance (direct reference to closing a window).

On the other hand, the expression of the force of an utterance may be quite indirect, often depending to a great extent on the context in which it occurs, particularly the relationship between the interlocutors and the situation in which they find themselves. Thus, an utterance used to perform a request may vary in directness from "Open the window please" (with an imperative illocutionary force indicating device) to "Could you open the window?" (using a conventionally indirect form with semantic content indicating the act) to "It's hot in here" (a somewhat opaque hint, if the intent of the speaker is that the hearer open the window). And in fact, an utterance with one surface illocutionary force can be used to perform an act with a different force if the circumstances and content are right. Consider the utterance "I promise I will never again borrow your car without asking you." Despite the presence of the performative verb *promise*, this utterance could be interpreted by an addressee and classified by a researcher as an apology, especially if the speaker had taken the addressee's car without permission.

Thus, the linguistic realization of an utterance (the form, the content, the surface illocutionary force), along with features of the situation in which the utterance is made, can be used to interpret or identify a speech act. Importantly, for the purposes of this book and, in general, in all work on cross-cultural speech acts, different cultures use different means to perform and interpret speech acts (see papers in Gass and Neu 1996).

In addition, the discourse context can be crucial in determining the force of an utterance. Because of the nature of refusals as face-threatening responding acts, many behaviors that could convey entirely different meanings (e.g., silence) may be interpreted as refusals when preceded by an interlocutor's request, invitation, offer, or suggestion. This sequential implicativeness results in a wide range of acts with varying degrees of indirectness being associated with refusal behavior. And indeed classifications of refusal acts reflect this fact. A look at some of the better known classification systems (see section 4.2) reveals that many acts are interpretable as refusals only if they are located directly after an appropriate initiating act.

Thus, it is perhaps not surprising that researchers who classify the realizations of a particular speech act frequently define their main set of categories in terms of the level of directness or transparency of the act. Blum-Kulka and Olshtain (1984: 201) identify the following three categories, based on level of directness, for analyzing requests:

1) most direct, explicit
2) conventional indirect
3) nonconventional indirect

Similarly, apologies are divided into two levels, according to their directness (p. 206).

1) most direct — utterances with an explicit illocutionary force indicating device
2) other — utterances whose semantic content is related to the preconditions on apologies

Using divisions based on degree of directness, researchers often code categories in terms of form, semantic content, or primary (superficial) illocutionary force. (See discussion in Blum-Kulka, House, and Kasper 1989: 275 on the need to use various aspects of language in the establishment of analytic categories.) In the next section we consider several classification systems that have been proposed for categorizing refusals.

4.2. *Classification systems*

A number of recent studies have investigated the realization of refusals across cultures. In this section we will concentrate on some of the systems proposed by different researchers for categorizing refusal strategies.

In a revised version of a (1976) article, Rubin (1983: 12-13) discusses the difficulty of recognizing the precise function of an act which may be associated with refusing. She sets out nine ways of saying *no*, which she claims are similar across a number of cultures. They include:

1. Be silent, hesitate, show a lack of enthusiasm
2. Offer an alternative
3. Postponement
4. Put the blame on a third party or something over which you have no control
5. Avoidance
6. General acceptance of an offer but giving no details
7. Divert and distract the addressee
8. General acceptance with excuses
9. Say what is offered is inappropriate

Rubin then notes that the fact that these ways of refusing ("forms," in Rubin's terms) may correspond from culture to culture does not indicate a correspondence of function. In fact, she argues that a person entering a culture must learn not only the forms associated with particular functions, but also the social factors and the underlying societal values involved in the appropriate performance of a particular act.

Another early attempt to capture how a refusal in a particular language can be effected is that of Ueda (1972: 189), who uses functions (e.g., apology, question), behavior (e.g., silence, exiting) and level of directness (e.g., vagueness), among other criteria, to describe how Japanese refuse. Ueda lists the following "16 ways to avoid saying no" in Japanese, several of which closely resemble Rubin's forms:

1. The equivalent of the English *no*
2. Vague *no*
3. Vague and ambiguous *yes* or *no*
4. Silence

5. Counter question
6. Tangential responses
7. Exiting
8. Lying, equivocation, etc.
9. Criticizing
10. Refusing the question
11. Conditional *no*
12. *Yes, but...*
13. Delaying answers
14. Internally *yes*, externally *no*
15. Internally *no*, externally *yes*
16. Apology

Ueda's categories are presented with little explanation as to how they were determined inasmuch as they were not based on data from her study (although after analyzing her data, Ueda appended an additional category, "Excuse — private reasons," to her list).   Ueda treats all 16 categories as possible Japanese responses.   However, when she applied these categories to 84 responses by adult Japanese men and women to 11 written dialogues, she noted that only 6 categories occurred regularly.[4]   Ueda found that, in general, Japanese tended to favor lying, equivocation as a way of refusing, avoiding reasons specifying why they were unable to give a positive response.[5]

Perhaps the best-known and most frequently cited system for analyzing refusals was developed by Beebe and her colleagues.   Although the system was presented in a paper by Beebe and Cummings (1985, published 1996) and used in an analysis by Takahashi and Beebe (1987), it is the paper by Beebe, Takahashi, and Uliss-Weltz (1990) which has attracted the most attention to this classification scheme.   Beebe, Takahashi, and Uliss-Weltz (1990: 72-73) break down refusal responses into semantic formulas[6] (those expressions which can be used to perform a refusal) and adjuncts (expressions which accompany a refusal, but which cannot by themselves be used to perform a refusal).   The semantic formulas and adjuncts are listed below:

Semantic formulas
  1. Direct
     a. Performative
     b. Nonperformative statement
  2. Indirect
     a. Statement of regret
     b. Wish
     c. Excuse, reason, explanation
     d. Statement of alternative
     e. Set condition for future or past acceptance
     f. Promise of future acceptance
     g. Statement of principle
     h. Statement of philosophy
     i. Attempt to dissuade interlocutor
     j. Acceptance that functions as a refusal
     k. Avoidance

Adjuncts
  1. Statement of positive opinion/feeling of agreement
  2. Statement of empathy
  3. Pause fillers
  4. Gratitude/appreciation

As might be expected, Beebe, Takahashi, and Uliss-Weltz's categories overlap to a great extent with Rubin's and Ueda's. However, this classification system differs as to its source in that the categories were established using data, primarily written responses to a discourse completion test, collected from native speakers of English, native speakers of Japanese, and native speakers of Japanese responding in English, supplemented by observations. There is clearly considerable advantage to grounding a classification system in data, as classes are based on real refusals. In addition, because of the nature of Beebe, Takahashi, and Uliss Weltz's data collection process, identification of the act was not in question.

Like Blum-Kulka and Olshtain (1984), Beebe, Takahashi, and Uliss-Weltz first divide the semantic formulas into direct and indirect realizations of refusals. Because the data used to determine the subcategories consist of responses to four different initiating acts (request, invitation, offer, and suggestion), a certain degree of generalizability is ensured.

On the other hand, it is not surprising that within the list of indirect refusals not only is there a wide range of frequently encountered possible responses represented, but semantic formulas are included which are associated in Beebe, Takahashi, and Uliss-Weltz's data with responses to only one or two of the initiating acts. Thus, the "statement of philosophy" category occurred in Beebe, Takahashi, and Uliss-Weltz's data only as a refusal to an offer (and to only one offer).

A consequence of basing the categories on data that, of necessity, represent a relatively limited number of responses is that as more data are collected, representing a wider sample of situations, nationalities, and data collection techniques, additional categories may be proposed. And in fact, researchers have argued for additional categories (Bardovi-Harlig and Hartford 1991; Houck and Gass 1996; Lyuh 1992; and Morrow 1995). (See also Chapter Two.)

The existence of a well thought out, well-defined classification system for refusals enables researchers to produce comparable analyses and results that are expressed in terms of the same categories. This is an advantage that has been put to use in recent research.

On the other hand, as more naturalistic data collection procedures have been employed, the problem mentioned in the previous section has had to be dealt with, that is, that the act being performed by a response is not always transparent. Ultimately, researchers have relied on several approaches (often associated with different data collection procedures) to determine the act being performed. In particular, access to the intentions of the refuser (e.g., through interview) and/or the response(s) of the refusee, in addition to the behavior of the refuser, is often used.

Access to the intentions of the Respondent is usually available in discourse completion tests in which the respondent is instructed beforehand to refuse. Thus, if a respondent has been told by a researcher to refuse and then produces a form of acceptance, the response is usually treated as a refusal. This is often the case with discourse completion tests, in which no immediate reaction by an Initiator is available. In situations in which the response is left up to the individual, researchers may interview participants to discuss their responses.

In recorded role plays or naturally occurring interactions, the behavior of an addressee (i.e., how an addressee reacts to a speaker's utterance) is often used to determine the force of the utterance. Thus, if an Initiator treats a half-hearted Acceptance by the Respondent as a Refusal, the act is categorized as a Refusal by the researcher (but see Goodwin and Goodwin 1987). In addition to access to linguistic forms, recorded data also allow researchers to use nonlinguistic aspects of utterances such as tone of voice. Even more information can be gleaned through video recordings inasmuch as they provide evidence of facial expressions, gestures, or posture, all of which may be used to determine what act has been performed and what the response to the act is.

5. Studies of refusals

In this section we discuss some of the results of research to date on the production of refusals. Perhaps the best-known refusal studies are those by Beebe and her colleagues — particularly studies by Takahashi and Beebe (1987) and by Beebe, Takahashi, and Uliss-Weltz (1990).

In their (1987) paper, Takahashi and Beebe attempted to discover, among other things, the amount of pragmatic transfer by native speakers of Japanese speaking English and the difference in amount of transfer by lower proficiency and higher proficiency non-native speakers. Takahashi and Beebe analyzed the written refusals of 20 native speakers of Japanese, 20 native speakers of English, 20 Japanese English as a foreign language (EFL) learners responding in English, and 20 Japanese English as a second language (ESL) learners also responding in English. The participants were asked to respond to situations described in a discourse completion test consisting of 12 written situations — 3 requests, 3 invitations, 3 offers, and 3 suggestions. The responses were analyzed according to the frequency, order, and content (or tone) of the semantic formulas and adjuncts. Takahashi and Beebe discovered transfer effects in the frequency and distribution of semantic formulas produced by the non-native speakers. They also showed that while transfer occurred among learners at both lower and higher levels of proficiency, learners at higher levels of proficiency tended to transfer more.

Beebe, Takahashi, and Uliss-Weltz (1990) considered the effects of pragmatic transfer in the responses of Japanese non-native speakers in a study somewhat similar to the (1987) study by Takahashi and Beebe. Using a design similar to that used by Takahashi and Beebe, they reported on data from three groups of native speakers of Japanese and English using a discourse completion test with 12 questions. In analyzing the results, the authors again considered the order, frequency, and content of the semantic formulas. Their results suggest evidence of pragmatic transfer, although they urge caution regarding the limitations of the data elicitation methods used. They found that Japanese sensitivity to status was reflected in differences between speech to superiors and subordinates, while American responses differed between status equals and status unequals; native speakers of Japanese and Japanese speakers using English used many more alternatives in general than native speakers of American English, as well as many more empathy adjuncts in a particularly delicate refusal of a request. And, the content of excuses by both Japanese using Japanese and Japanese using English tended to be less specific and more formal. The similarities between Japanese using Japanese and Japanese responding in English, when contrasted with the responses of native speakers of English, lend strong support to claims of the pervasiveness of pragmatic transfer.

Other studies have focused on different questions regarding non-native refusal production. For instance, in their work on academic advising sessions, Bardovi-Harlig and Hartford (1991) compared the semantic formulas used by native speakers and non-native speakers of English in refusing an advisor's suggestion. They were particularly interested in the extent to which non-native rejections deviated from those of native speakers. Bardovi-Harlig and Hartford examined tape recordings of actual advising sessions and, using Beebe, Takahashi, and Uliss-Weltz's taxonomy, identified and classified students' rejections. While their analysis indicates that reasons/explanations were the semantic formula most frequently used by both native speakers and non-native speakers, the second most common strategy among native speakers was alternatives, while among non-native speakers, it was avoidance. Bardovi-Harlig and Hartford note that even though reasons were employed frequently by native speakers and non-native speakers, the range of content of non-native speakers' reasons was broader and more often unacceptable. Thus, the semantic formulas that native speakers and non-native speaker used in rejecting their advisors' advice differed both quantitatively and qualitatively.

Morrow (1995) also compared non-native and native speaker refusals. In a study designed to investigate the effects of instruction on non-native speakers' refusal and complaint production, Morrow collected role play data from native and non-native speakers of English using four situations involving friends and acquaintances. Analysis of the refusal data showed, among other things, that non-native speakers tended to be less indirect, invoked fewer positive and more negative politeness strategies, and offered fewer explanations and excuses than did native speakers. After instruction, non-native speakers used fewer inappropriate semantic formulas and increased their use of positive politeness forms. In other words, they moved closer to production that is typical of American English.

While the previous studies investigated characteristics of non-native speaker refusals in English, some studies have focused only on refusals in a particular culture, often with an eye to linking a preference for particular semantic formulas or linguistic modifications to characteristics of the culture or society. Chen, Ye, and Zhang (1995) collected data from 100 native speakers of Mandarin Chinese (using a questionnaire similar to Beebe, Takahashi, and Uliss-Weltz's) to determine the most frequently used strategies in refusal situations by speakers of Mandarin Chinese. They divided refusals into substantive (those in which a refusal is intended) and ritual (a polite act indicating the refuser's concern for the person doing the offering or inviting). Chen, Ye, and Zhang employed Beebe, Takahashi, and Uliss-Weltz's classification system in determining that the main strategies used by native speakers of Mandarin for substantive refusals were reasons, followed by alternatives. They noted that the former allow the refuser to justify the refusal without threatening face, while the latter enable the refuser to avoid confrontation.

In another investigation of Mandarin Chinese refusals, focusing primarily on politeness aspects, Liao (1994) used a number of elicitation techniques (interviews, evaluations of Rubin's strategies by native speakers of Mandarin, participant observations, realistic conversation writing, discourse completion tests, and native speaker intuitions) to ascertain modes of refusal among over 1000 adults and more than 500 children. Liao created her own list of refusal strategies, a composite of those suggested by Rubin and those suggested by Beebe, Takahashi, and Uliss-Weltz, Ueda, as well as others. Her results led her to observe that while the strategies suggested by other researchers as universal occur in Mandarin, the content of these strategies, particularly the use of conventionalized responses and the different degrees of politeness employed in different circumstances, is culture specific.

In a similar vein, a study of Japanese was undertaken in which characteristics of Japanese refusals were directly contrasted with those of English refusals. Kinjo (1987) examined refusals to invitations and requests in English and Japanese. Data were collected orally, with 30 native English and 30 native Japanese subjects responding to 20 taped invitations or requests in an oral version of a discourse completion test. Kinjo used elements of Takahashi and Beebe's (1987) classification system to analyze the discourse components of participants' responses. She found similarities in the frequency of use of particular formulas by both groups; however, there was wide variation in the ordering of discourse components according to individual and situation. In her analysis, Kinjo also considered the distribution of mitigators and the degree to which directness or indirectness reflected stereotypical notions of these two cultures. From a linguistic standpoint, she found that American females used "I'm sorry" more frequently than American males, while Japanese, both male and female, used the expression with similar frequencies and that Americans used intensifiers in their responses to everyone, while Japanese used them only to someone they liked. Sociocultural analysis revealed Japanese as being more open and direct, perhaps because the role plays were set up as conversations between equals. As with the Beebe, Takahashi, and Uliss-Weltz study, Kinjo warns that the results that come about as a result of this method may not reflect naturally occurring speech.

Thus, while a wide range of research has been and is being carried out describing refusals within cultures, comparing refusals across cultures, and contrasting native and non-native refusals, analysis has focused primarily on the acts or strategies used to perform a refusal. As mentioned earlier, in this book we will be looking at what can be discovered by going beyond linguistic analyses of individual refusal turns and focusing on aspects of both verbal and nonverbal interaction in refusal sequences in which non-native speakers (native speakers of Japanese in the present research) interact with native speakers of English.

Specifically, in the remainder of the book we will first discuss different methodologies for collecting data and their effects on the interpretation of that data. This includes a proposal of additional category types (Chapter Two) and a recommendation for a unit of analysis for extended refusal interactions (the episode) and the analysis of a complex refusal interaction sequence (Chapter Three). We will then look at the management of back channel type utterances (Chapter Four) and nonverbal behavior (Chapter Five) by non-native speakers, and the role of non-native speaker interactive behaviors as communication strategies (Chapter Six). We will consider the role of the native speaker in the formulation of appropriate non-native speaker responses (Chapter Seven) and we relate the behaviors that we have observed to issues in language learning (Chapter Eight). Finally, in Chapter Nine, we provide a brief overview of the main findings of the refusals examined in this book.

Chapter 2
Issues of methodology

1. Introduction

The concern with methodology has been and continues to be central in second language research (see for example the series on research methodology by Gass and Schachter [Chaudron, in preparation; Duff, in preparation; Gass and Mackey, in preparation; Harrington, in preparation; Kasper and Rose, in preparation; Markee, in preparation; Yule 1997]).

Before proceeding, we want to eliminate any possible confusion about the scope of the research reported in this book. In general, the literature refers to a broad area of research known as second language acquisition. Second language acquisition encompasses a wide range of activities and, in fact, is often practiced by individuals who approach the field with different academic backgrounds and orientations. This diversity has been noted by many, including Gass and Selinker (1994: 1), who attempt to characterize the many facets of the field of second language acquisition.

> [Second language acquisition] is the study of how second languages are learned. It is the study of how learners create a new language system with only limited exposure to a second language. It is the study of what is learned of a second language and what is not learned; it is the study of why most second language learners do not achieve the same degree of proficiency in a second language as they do in their native language: it is also the study of why only some learners appear to achieve native-like proficiency in more than one language. Additionally, second language acquisition is concerned with the nature of the hypotheses (whether conscious or unconscious) that learners come up with regarding the rules of the second language. Are the rules like those of the native language? Are they like the rules of the language being learned? Are there patterns that are common to all learners regardless of the native language and regardless of the language being learned? Do the rules created by second language learners vary according to the context of use?

As is apparent, there are many ways of approaching the field of second language acquisition. The central question, however, relates to how nonprimary acquisition takes place.

In an attempt to disambiguate the varied research agenda that fall under the umbrella of Second Language Acquisition, Gass (1995, 1998) and Seliger (1983) suggested a different terminology with which to characterize the broad field of research on non-native speaker language: Second Language Studies. This terminology has the advantage of addressing other questions in addition to that of how nonprimary acquisition takes place Within the category of second language studies (but not necessarily of second language acquisition) are included areas of research such as discourse analysis, speech acts, and communication strategies, all of which deal with non-native speaker language in use. This is not to say that these areas are not part of the study of acquisition, but it must be demonstrated that they are directly related to how second languages are learned. This relationship is diagrammed in Figure 3.

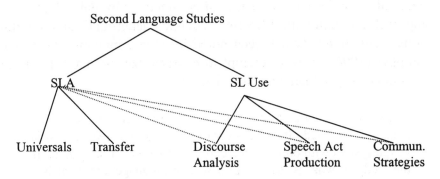

Figure 3. A characterization of research in "Second Language Studies"

The dotted lines indicate a more tenuous relationship, one that needs to be argued rather than accepted *a priori.*

The distinction that we are making is not unlike one made by Færch and Kasper (1987), who refer to the broader area of second language research rather than to second language acquisition, thereby distinguishing between second language acquisition and second language use (the primary topic of this book).

2. Data collection

Since the inception of second language studies (of which second language acquisition and second language use are integral parts, as mentioned above), researchers have recognized the special role of methodology and the accompanying vexing questions of analysis and interpretation. In this chapter we focus on the issue of data collection in the hope of elucidating methodological issues in nonnative speech act research. Many scholars have emphasized the point, with which we concur, that methodological issues cannot be ignored; for it is not clear to what extent differences in methodology yield differences in results (see, for example, Cohen 1996; Cohen and Olshtain 1994; Rose 1992, 1994; Rose and Ono 1995).

In trying to understand the nature of human behavior, we are always faced with a lack of consistency in our observations. That is, observing behavior in what appears to be the same situation rarely brings consistent results. Language behavior, as one aspect of human behavior, is no exception. Lack of consistency in research findings is generally compensated by use of a large numbers of subjects; one is then often able to discern trends. In fact, a number of years ago, in looking at the role of language transfer in second language acquisition, Gass (1984) noted that one can only expect to find probabilistic results. Absoluteness in acquisition and use is rarely, if ever, the norm.

Acceptance of probabilistic predictions and probabilistic results is necessary to the development of our understanding of how second languages are learned and of how second languages are used. This is the case in part because no two linguistic situations are identical, and with regard to sociolinguistic research, no two sociolinguistic situations are the same. That is, no two individuals structure their knowledge of their first and second languages in exactly the same way; and no two individuals find themselves in the same social situation (i.e., with all the same variables of speaker, hearer, age, gender, setting, topic, prior experiences, etc.). Further, no single individual finds herself in the same social situation twice. This has led to the well-known research findings concerning variation both across subjects and within subjects.

This being a fact of life that we need to deal with, how can we ever obtain results from research on second language acquisition and use that can reliably form the basis of theories? As mentioned, one way is through the use of large numbers of subjects to discern prob- abilistic trends. While this is perhaps ideal, it is generally not prac- tical given the kinds of methods that are generally employed.

In early work within the tradition of speech acts Wolfson (1981) and Wolfson, Marmor, and Jones (1989) argued that ethnographic data collection is the most reliable means of learning about the social and linguistic constraints on a particular speech act. This methodol- ogy allows for observation of naturally occurring speech events with precise recording about the social setting, location, and participants, thereby providing information about the linguistic and social use of a given speech act (cf. Watson-Gegeo 1988 for a discussion of methodological issues). Beebe (1993) has followed this line of rea- soning and has developed what she terms notebook data (1994) as a means of ensuring that the necessary sociolinguistic data surround- ing a speech act are available.[7] However, while questions of validity may be satisfied, reliability remains an issue.

A strand of research that attempts to bring together some of the advantages of naturalistic data with the advantages of sociolinguistic controls (in this case setting, and perhaps event) is seen in work by Bardovi-Harlig and Hartford (1991), who collected office hour data in an American university from native speaker and non-native speaker students in sessions with their academic advisors. Similarly, work by Fiksdal (1990) examined advising sessions between non- native speakers (students) and advisors, the latter with expertise in immigration matters. However, while both of these pieces of re- search involved data collection procedures which enabled the re- searchers to control the topic and setting to some degree, and to gather data in a reasonably naturalistic setting, it is also apparent that not all social variables could be controlled for.

The controversy surrounding data collection is, of course, not unique to sociolinguistic data. For example, researchers dealing with second language acquisition studies relying on acceptability judgments such as Goss, Zhang, and Lantolf (1994) argue that the issue of validity is a central one, whereas Gass (1994), also dealing with acceptability judgments, counters that reliability is no less im- portant, and that both need to be examined in tandem.[8]

As has been pointed out by a number of researchers studying cross-cultural speech acts (e.g., Bardovi-Harlig and Hartford 1992; Kasper and Dahl 1991; Rintell and Mitchell 1989), there are limitations to the benefits of ethnographic research. Two are noteworthy: 1) as mentioned above, contextual variables cannot be controlled; and 2) the occurrence of a particular speech act cannot be predicted. This latter is important since if one is truly to understand a given speech act, many occurrences are needed. It is, of course, difficult to ensure large numbers of instances of a speech act when one must rely on spontaneous occurrences of the act in natural interaction.

In the most detailed treatment to date on the issue of methodology in second language speech act research, Kasper and Dahl (1991) reviewed 39 studies of interlanguage pragmatics. They characterized the methods used along two dimensions: 1) the constraints that each imposes on the data and 2) the degree to which production or comprehension is studied. For our purposes, we focus only on production data, although we bear in mind Kasper's (1984) caution that many apparent production problems, at least with non-native speakers of a language, are a result of a non-native speaker's inadequate comprehension of previous parts of the discourse.

Focusing on production data, Kasper and Dahl describe two major data elicitation measures: discourse completion tests and role plays.[9] Discourse completion tests are written questionnaires comprising a brief description of a situation followed by dialogue with a blank line (or lines) where the subject is to write what she or he believes to be an appropriate response (see section 2.1). The other major type of elicited production data comes from role plays, both open and closed. Closed role plays are exemplified in a study by Rintell and Mitchell (1989), in which subjects were given an oral version of the discourse completion test and had one "turn" in which to respond orally. In open role plays, on the other hand, an entire dialogue is observed and recorded. In the next two sections we review recent studies that have focused on the methodological constraints of these two data elicitation measures. Then, in section 2.3, we review research dealing with comparisons of multiple elicitation types.

2.1. *Discourse completion tests*

The practical questions of reliability can in part be resolved through the collection of large amounts of data. This has in fact been done in the area of speech act research through the well-known discourse completion test. A discourse completion test is a pencil and paper task that requires subjects to write what they believe they would say in a particular context. In most tasks a situation is described (e.g., an important client invites a salesperson to dinner at a restaurant where the salesperson's ex-boyfriend works), blank lines are drawn for the response, and (sometimes) a follow-up response is provided such as "That's too bad, maybe some other time," which strongly suggests the content of the response to be filled in.

There are advantages and disadvantages to this type of data collection. The advantages are clear: Large amounts of data can be collected in a relatively short amount of time and from respondents with a wide range of individual characteristics. Furthermore, because of the consistency of the situation, responses can be compared along a number of dimensions (e.g., age, gender, ethnicity). On the other hand, disadvantages are noteworthy. There is the question of the extent to which the data collected actually reflect the sociolinguistic constraints that operate on the speech act in question in natural circumstances. This is argued by Wolfson, Marmor, and Jones (1989: 182), who point out that "short decontextualized written segments" may not be comparable to what takes place in actual interaction.

In fact, recent research on the comparability of discourse completion test data with data collected using other techniques has revealed some important differences. Rose (1992, 1994) and Rose and Ono (1995) have shown that the frequency of different types of response varies with the instrument. Rose (1994) compared requests elicited by a discourse completion test with responses to a multiple choice questionnaire, both of which were administered in English to native speakers of English and in Japanese to native speakers of Japanese. He reports that while the most frequent response to all situations was conventionally indirect requests, responses to the multiple choice questionnaire exhibited more contextual variation, with respondents often choosing to opt out or to hint. Similar results were obtained in a study by Rose and Ono (1995), who, with situations more appropriate to a Japanese context, compared the two elicitation types using Japanese subjects. The results from most of the 12 situations used by Rose and Ono differed depending on the elicitation measure. For example, opting out and hinting occurred more frequently with the multiple choice questionnaires than with the discourse completion tests. Both the Rose and the Rose and Ono studies call into question the validity of discourse completion tests, particularly in a non-western context.

On the other hand, written and oral versions (sometimes referred to as closed role plays) of the same discourse completion test have produced comparable results. Turnbull (1994) compared two ways of eliciting data using discourse completion tests: oral and written. In the written discourse completion test, the standard format of writing responses was used (although the initial request was made orally); in the oral version, the subjects listened to a tape and provided an oral response. The results suggested little difference in the oral versus written format, although it is important to note that both oral and written tests generated what Turnbull argues are simplified data and hence potentially nonrepresentational.

Rintell and Mitchell (1989) also used written and oral versions of the same discourse completion test (eliciting apologies and requests), which were given to low advanced learners of English and to native English speakers. The researcher explained the situation orally to the participants, who then were given an unlimited amount of time to respond orally. A variety of social roles and situations were represented. Clearly some differences did exist between the two modalities of elicitation. In particular, for the second language speakers, the oral data were longer than the written data. This difference was not apparent in the native English speaker responses, leading the authors to conclude that it was not so much the methodology that resulted in different responses, but rather the way in which the two groups approached the tasks. In general they found that the "language elicited...is very similar whether collected in written or oral form" (p. 270). They argue that the discourse completion test is in actuality a role play. That is, both the written and spoken forms provide data that resemble spoken language rather than written language.

Thus, research comparing data from discourse completion tests with data from multiple-choice questionnaires indicates that there are often important differences in results obtained from different written instruments. However, investigations of results from different versions of the discourse completion test (e.g., oral versus written) have revealed little variation. In the next section we will consider studies that have compared results from open role plays with data from discourse completion tests.

2.2. *Role play*

Role plays have the advantage of providing data in an oral mode rather than a written mode (although, as discussed above, discourse completion tests can be conducted in an oral mode as well). Two general types of role play are referred to in the literature: closed role plays and open role plays. As explained in section 2.1, closed role plays are in actuality an oral version of the discourse completion test. In a closed role play (e.g., Walters 1980), subjects are given a situation and are asked to give a one-turn oral response. However, as pointed out above, any type of elicitation procedure that is closed, in that it does not allow a free range of answers or interaction, is likely to suffer from the possibility of non-symmetry with naturally occurring data.

Open role plays involve interaction played out by two (or more) interactants in response to a situation posited by the researcher. In this section we focus on two studies investigating the effectiveness of open role plays, as opposed to discourse completion tests, in collecting data on refusals. In his study of refusals, in addition to discourse completion tests, Turnbull (1994) also used open role plays and actual telephone calls. In the role play situation, participants received a pretend telephone call (the participants were sitting on either side of a low screen) and were asked to role play a response. In his comparison of role plays (and relatively natural telephone calls [the request was scripted, but the responses were not]) with discourse completion tests, Turnbull shows that the results from both oral and written discourse completion tests differed greatly from data obtained from open role plays and from naturally occurring data both in the distribution of types of acts and in the internal structure of the acts. Comparing open role plays and naturally occurring data, Turnbull noted that role plays are similar in many respects to naturally occurring data, although they tend to be more rambling and repetitive, that is, it may be more difficult to put closure on a role play request as opposed to a true request.

Sasaki (1998) also compared refusals elicited by discourse completion tests with open role play data. She likewise found differences in terms of response length and content (semantic formulas used), as well as native speaker evaluation of the responses. Both Sasaki and Turnbull argue (and the results from data reported in this book corroborate their argument) that the differences they found relate to the interactive nature of the role play task as opposed to the more static nature of the discourse completion test. The latter does not adequately represent what goes on in an interactive refusal encounter.

Thus, of the common data elicitation methods, open role plays seem the closest to what we might expect to reflect naturally occurring speech events. As Kasper and Dahl (1991) note, open role plays represent "full operation of the turn-taking mechanism, impromptu planning decisions contingent on interlocutor input, and hence, negotiation of global and local goals" (p. 228), as well as the sequential organization of speech act performance and the kinds of responses that specific choices evoke. In addition, they have the advantage of allowing the researcher to set up situations in which the occurrence of a particular speech act is likely, thereby ensuring the occurrence of the act under study in the presence of a tape recorder and/or a video camera.

However, open role plays are not problem free. They are cumbersome to administer and time-consuming in both their administration and analysis. Furthermore, role plays are just that, role plays, with few, if any, real or real life consequences. So again, we are left with the question of the degree to which role plays really mirror the linguistic behavior of individuals in the particular setting established by the researcher.

2.3. *Other methodology comparisons*

We turn now to a discussion of the literature in which methodological comparisons are made. We focus here on methodologies that involve data collection techniques other than discourse completion tests and role plays. In addition to Kasper and Dahl's (1991) survey on methodological issues, there are a number of other studies that present results based on a comparison of methodologies (some of which have been discussed in the preceding sections on discourse completion tests and role plays). We will focus primarily on those studying the speech act of refusal.

Some of the most interesting studies involve comparisons of discourse completion tests with naturally occurring data. Beebe and Cummings (1996) studied refusals using two types of data for their analysis: real telephone requests and a discourse completion test based on these requests. Data were collected only from native speakers of English. In both the written and the oral tasks, subjects were asked if they would be willing to help with the local arrangements for the upcoming TESOL (Teachers to Speakers of Other Languages) convention, which was to be held in New York.

What Beebe and Cummings found was that in the oral data there was more elaboration of the refusal; in the written data, the layout on the page allowed for only a minimum amount of data to be produced. Elaborations came as a result of the requester's response (see Figure 2, Chapter One). If the requester, upon hearing a refusal, responded "all right, thank you" and then hung up, there was no further need for elaboration. But if, on the other hand, there was silence or an attempt to keep the conversation going, the refuser elaborated, perhaps so as not to be offensive to the requester. Goffman (1971) notes that the offending person (in this case the refuser) needs to receive reassurance from the addressee (who is the requester) that his/her offending remark is not taken as a serious offense. Elaboration is what restores the offender to his/her proper place in the eyes of the addressee. Beebe and Cummings (1985: 4) point out that the written tests bias results in many ways, specifically because of "less negotiation, less hedging, less repetition, less elaboration, less variety, and less talk."

Beebe and Cummings analyzed the written and oral data in terms of the types of responses given, finding that the written data reflect the content of oral data (e.g., the use of "I'm sorry," the frequency with which excuses were offered, and the frequency with which willingness or ability was mentioned). Where the two modes differed was in what they call the *psychosocial* domain. That is, when one refuses, one needs to take a cue from the requester as to how offensive or how important the refusal is. This will then dictate the degree to which further elaboration, hedging, or apologizing is necessary. Thus, the interlocutor was crucial in determining how a refusal developed.

The elaborate nature of spontaneously produced refusals has been further pointed out by Hartford and Bardovi-Harlig (1992). They compared semantic formulas resulting from naturally occurring data with those elicited by a discourse completion test. Data were collected in an institutional setting in which the interactants and situations are relatively invariant. The interactions were audiotaped, and participants were aware of being observed and recorded. Their analysis focused on rejections of advice in academic advising sessions. The eight discourse completion tests developed for comparison were based on data from these sessions. They included situations which were frequent in the advising sessions with non-native students, but rarely occurred with native speaker students.

Hartford and Bardovi-Harlig discovered a number of differences between data from the discourse completion tests and the real advising sessions. They found that the most frequent strategies used in responses to the discourse completion tests differed from the most frequent strategies in the naturally occurring data: 1) a number of common semantic formulas in real advising sessions did not occur in responses to discourse completion tests and 2) semantic formulas that occurred in the discourse completion test data did not occur in the advising sessions. In addition, while in both discourse completion tests and natural advising sessions non-native speakers exhibited what Hartford and Bardovi-Harlig called *verbal avoidance*, two manifestations frequently found in the natural data did not occur in the discourse completion tests: requests for repetition ("Which one was that one?") and requests for additional information ("Do you know anything about 560, uh um, who teaches?") (pp. 42-43).

Hartford and Bardovi-Harlig concluded that discourse completion tests result in limited data; specifically, their results showed a more · limited range of semantic formulas, fewer status-preserving strategies, and, of course, none of the extended negotiations that occurred in the natural data. Clearly, written responses, especially those that are sandwiched between an opening statement and a follow-up statement (as in many discourse completion tests), do not allow a speaker to exhibit the full range of response types that are found in naturalistic data. This does not necessarily suggest an overall superiority for the collection of naturally occurring data since the sheer quantity of data that can be elicited through some sort of forced elicitation measure allows for the testing of hypotheses, which is not possible when data are sporadic and uncontrolled. As Bardovi-Harlig and Hartford (1990) note, combinations of data elicitation methods are necessary for the generation, testing, and substantiation of hypotheses about non-native speech act behavior.

Other research on methodology has focused on multi-method comparison. Yamashita (1996) investigated testing instruments for the assessment of pragmatic knowledge of English native speakers learning Japanese. Six tests were used, including 1) a self-assessment, 2) an oral production test, 3) an open discourse completion test, 4) a role play 5) a role play self-assessment, and 6) a multiple choice discourse completion test.

In the self-assessment, learners were presented with a situation (written format), as in a discourse completion test, and were asked to think about what they would say in Japanese in such a situation and then to rate their ability to respond appropriately in that situation. In the oral production test (an oral discourse completion test), learners listened to a tape in which a situation was described, after which they responded orally to the situation. The open discourse completion test used a written format, both in the presentation of the situation and in the response requested. The role play was an oral video-taped session in which participants acted out their responses to the scenario presented. After learners participated in the role play, they provided a self-assessment of their ability to respond appropriately. Thus, the role play itself provided two measures of assessment (the role play and the self-assessment of the performance of the role play). The final measure used a multiple choice format. Situations just like the ones in the discourse completion tests were presented with three possible responses from which subjects had to select one.

The results of this multiple-method comparison suggest that with the exception of the multiple choice instrument, all methods are reliable and valid. Further, issues such as proficiency and exposure to the target culture are related to some measures, but not others. In particular, a relationship exists between length of exposure to the L2 and the two oral production tests (oral production and role play) and between proficiency and the three production tests (oral production, role play, and open discourse completion test).

Yamashita's study was based on work by Hudson, Detmer, and Brown (1992, 1995), whose main interest was a comparison of methods for evaluating pragmatic competence with a focus on reliability and validity. Among the variables that were of issue were power, relationship (i.e., distance), and the degree of imposition of the speech act. Of particular relevance to the present study, which uses role plays as the basis for data elicitation, is Hudson, Detmer, and Brown's discussion of the development and format of role plays (1995: 59-60). Hudson, Detmer, and Brown list five design considerations for role plays:

1. A person in addition to the researcher should be used to avoid the overlap of researcher and role play roles.
2. A situation should not place too much burden in terms of conceptualization and actualization.
3. Action should be kept to a minimum and should not involve drama to a large extent.
4. Action scenarios at the expense of scenarios requiring language should be avoided.
5. Props may be helpful.

These considerations were also important in the establishment of the role play situations in the data presented here, as well as in the establishment of our data collection procedures.

3. Video data

In addition to issues of data elicitation, we considered the importance of visual access to the data we collected. In research on second language acquisition and second language use, video is not the norm. To the contrary, it is rarely used as a means of data collection. Within the context of speech act research, this may partly be due to the fact that there has been an emphasis on either discourse completion tests, where clearly video data are superfluous, or spontaneously produced speech, where video data cannot be planned (assuming, of course, that researchers do not happen to carry a video camera with them at all times). Video, however, can clearly cause an adjustment in our perceptions of the speech event and in some instances constrain the interpretation of the linguistic data.

In this chapter, after a description of the data-base used in this book (section 4), we present a discussion of how the interactions that occur in an open role play can lead to additional insights into the linguistic resources that non-native speakers bring to bear on the act of refusal (section 5). We then present preliminary examples of how nonverbal data can have a significant impact on the interpretation of second language linguistic data (section 6).

4. Data-base

In the preceding sections we have discussed many of the advantages and disadvantages of various research methodologies. Because our research had as its major focus a detailed treatment of refusal interactions, it was necessary to select a methodology that would allow for data that was controlled in terms of the content and natural in terms of the interaction. In addition, we wanted access to visual as well as audio aspects of the interactions in order to examine both verbal and nonverbal data.

With the caveats in mind concerning role plays (see section 2.2), the data discussed in this book come from open role plays. We made this choice fully aware of the disadvantages, but also aware of the advantages, particularly with regard to refusals. As Edmondson (1981) points out, some speech acts do not result from only one utterance; rather they are a product of negotiation involving two speakers. As he states, many speech acts "are not meant to be determinate, their significance is negotiable" (pp. 29-30). It is clear that to see this type, as well as other types, of negotiation in refusals, an open format to elicit data was required.

In our attempt to investigate interlanguage refusals, we were primarily concerned with the interaction involved in the refusal itself. Refusals are played out events, rather than instances characterized by a brief exchange or single utterance. That is, we begin with the notion that any delimited elicitation (e.g., discourse completion test, closed role play) is insufficient to an understanding of the complete speech event of refusing.

Following the work of Beebe, Takahashi, and Uliss-Weltz (1990), we investigated refusals to four types of situations: 1) suggestions, 2) offers, 3) invitations, and 4) requests. We departed from most previous studies of refusals in two ways: 1) we used videotaped data, and 2) we used full role play situations, which allow participants to carry out the refusal to its logical conclusion.[10] Importantly, the responses were not confined either by the printed page (e.g., the amount of space provided on the page, the number of turns that the respondent is expected to take) or by the closing response of the initiator of the interaction, which in many discourse completion tests directs the refusal by sandwiching it between a given opening remark and the subsequent closing comment. In other words, respondents to a discourse completion test know the precise outcome before they know how they will get to the outcome. This was not the case in the role plays from which our data were collected.

Two situations requiring refusals were created for each of the four refusal types mentioned above so that a total of eight situations existed (see Appendix I). In defining the setting for the role plays, we opted for what Trosborg (1995: 144, citing McDonough 1981) refers to as *role enactment* ("performing a role that is part of one's normal life or personality"), rather than *role play* ("pretending to react as if one were someone else in a different situation"). The setting for each was the home of an American host family who asked the guest to do something undesirable such as go skydiving, get a strange haircut, give a speech at church, or pierce his/her ears. The data were collected immediately following an actual home-stay weekend in which the non-native speakers had visited an American family. One could argue that it is highly unlikely that a non-native speaker would encounter situations such as the ones used in this study. However, this appears not to be the case. Some of these situations had quite coincidentally been encountered, as had even more bizarre ones, such as a suggestion to go to the morgue to see a body.

Each role play consists of an interaction involving a native speaker of English, who was the person making the request, invitation, suggestion, or offer, and a Japanese non-native speaker of English at a low to intermediate level of proficiency (proficiency levels were determined by the participants' placement in one of two levels in their English program). The non-native speakers were young adults who were in the United States for a brief period of study. They had been in the country for less than a month and intended to return to Japan within a few weeks following the data collection.

Participants in the study were given the contextual information surrounding each situation. We made certain that they understood the situation before the session began. The non-native speakers were not instructed on how to respond. Following the explanation of the situation, each subject role played with a native speaker who had been instructed not to give up too easily in cases in which the non-native speaker initially refused. All sessions were videotaped.

For each of the 8 situations, data from at least three non-native speaker-native speaker interactions were gathered. A total of 24 useable role plays were videotaped. Of these, 23 achieved a resolution (one ended in communication breakdown): 15 resulted in a Final Outcome of Nonaccept, where Nonaccept includes refusal or alternative and 8 resulted in an Accept (conditional or nonconditional).

5. Analysis of interactional aspects — Effect of open role play

The data we collected using an open role play differed from data collected using a written or tape-recorded elicitation instrument in a number of significant ways. The most obvious was the dynamic nature of the interaction resulting from a real face-to-face encounter. It is one thing to formulate a refusal on paper; it is quite another to deliver that refusal to a person who will respond to it. Not once in our data did the refusal interaction terminate with the subject's initial response.[11] The role plays resulted in what were often lengthy inter-actions in which the participants negotiated their way to a resolution. During this time, speakers hemmed and hawed, cut each other off, requested clarification, self corrected, modified and elaborated their positions, and generally became involved in negotiating semantic, pragmatic, and social meaning.[12] Thus, our role play data differ from most other data on refusals both quantitatively and qualita-tively (but see Bardovi-Harlig and Hartford 1991; Morrow 1995 for important exceptions).

5.1. *Quantitative analysis*

Because our concern is with the shape of negotiated interactions in a refusal encounter, the bulk of this book focuses on qualitative analy-ses of these interactions. However, to frame the discussion, we be-gin with a brief quantitative analysis. One quantitative consequence of using an open role play is that the data consist not of one re-sponse, but rather of a series of turns. To obtain a quantitative measure of the data, we considered turn length and number of turns from a subset of the data (excluding situations one and two). Turn length often varied according to level of English ability (see also Blum-Kulka and Olshtain 1986), with less proficient subjects fre-quently producing shorter turns. After eliminating back channels, such as *mm* and *oh*, and pause fillers, such as *uh*, we found that sub-jects with lower English proficiency averaged approximately 3.5 words per turn. Higher proficiency subjects were much more pro-lific, averaging approximately 10.7 words per turn.[13]

We also looked at the number of turns. As reported earlier, Beebe and Cummings (1996) note that the number of turns is strongly influenced by the interlocutor's response. The figures re-ported here should be interpreted with this in mind. In our data, the total number of turns from the triggering speech act to the end of the role play generally varied between 7 and 18, with a few exception-ally long interactions such as the one analyzed in this chapter. On the average, subjects required 9.8 turns at talk to reach a resolution.[14]

As might be expected with real negotiations, the outcomes differed considerably. Resolution was achieved when the participants reached agreement and 1) the native speaker accepted the non-native speaker's refusal (or postponement), or 2) the native speaker and non-native speaker agreed on an alternative activity. As mentioned above, both of these are treated as Nonaccepts. Resolution could also be reached if 3) the non-native speaker accepted the native speaker's offer, request, invitation, or suggestion. Acceptance could be total or conditional.

5.2. *Qualitative analysis: Classifying the data*

We also analyzed the refusal sequences, categorizing the responses made by the non-native speakers. As a starting point, we applied the classification system developed by Beebe, Takahashi, and Uliss-Weltz (1990) to each non-native speaker response (see Chapter One). Application of Beebe, Takahashi, and Uliss-Weltz's classification system to interactional data has some obvious disadvantages. Paramount is the fact that the system was developed for single turn responses, in which one act was identified as the head act and any other language was analyzed as a supportive move. In our analysis, we applied the classification to all the acts that could be argued to be directly involved in negotiating the refusal. This sometimes resulted in several acts in the same turn being treated as refusal strategies. On the other hand, the advantage of using this system was that by relying on the most widely used refusal classification system, we intended that our findings would be comparable to those of a large number of other researchers.

The following strategies occurred in our data.

1. Conventional nonperformative refusal (e.g., "I can't"; "no")
2. Statement of regret (e.g., "I'm sorry")
3. Excuse/reason/explanation (e.g., "but I don't know you")[15]
4. Proposal of alternative (e.g., "please wait in your car if you want to meet him")
5. Attempt to Dissuade Interlocutor (e.g., Negative consequence — "it is bad for you")

Originally, we included *postponement* as a subcategory of avoidance. In a number of instances, the refuser cited some vague future time at which s/he might undertake the action (e.g., "I want to pierce my ears but mm someday"). However, since there was little chance that the refuser would be in the United States when this occurred, these instances functioned more as reasons for not performing the act at that time than as postponements, as proposed by Beebe, Takahashi, and Uliss-Weltz (Beebe, personal communication). In addition, occasionally an alternative such as "please wait in your car if you want to meet him" would ultimately result in the requested act (entrance to the house) being accomplished. However, since the speaker was not in a position to grant the request at any time, we treated this as an alternative, rather than a postponement.

Numbers 1-4 accounted for approximately two-thirds of the responses. These responses also predominate in data from other research on refusals, such as the studies by Bardovi-Harlig and Hartford (1990), Kinjo (1987), and Morrow (1995).

Adjuncts which occurred in our study were:

1. Statements of empathy
2. Pause fillers
3. Expressions of gratitude

However, our data also contained non-native speaker responses that did not fit neatly within the Beebe, Takahashi, and Uliss-Weltz classification system. Three of these were linguistic responses: 1) confirmations, 2) requests for clarification/information, and 3) agreements. We deal with these in the next three sections. A fourth type of response, nonverbal messages, will be discussed in section 6.1 and examined more extensively in Chapter Four.

5.2.1. Confirmation

Confirmations occurred frequently in the conversations of lower-proficiency non-native speakers. When a non-native speaker began groping for words (perhaps a signal for help) or exhibiting signs of linguistic distress, the native speaker often leapt in, checking assumptions and elaborating on minimal utterances. The non-native speaker could then respond with a single word, indicating that the native speaker was correct. The non-native speaker was thus able to get away with a minimum amount of speech, as in Example (6), where he is a guest at a weekend home-stay. At breakfast, the native speaker is inviting him to go skydiving with the family that day. (Transcription conventions are presented in Appendix II).

(6)   Confirmation (skydiving)[16]

	1	NS:	do you like to skydive?
	2	NNS:	no
	3	NS:	no?
→	4	NNS:	NOD yes NOD
	5	NS:	why
	6	NNS:	uh I head(eh) headek headache
	7	NS:	y have...headache?
→	8	NNS:	headache
	9	NS:	oh you have a headache oh no he has a headache
→	10	NNS:	headache

In line 2 the non-native speaker indicates his lack of interest in skydiving, and in line 4 he confirms it with a single word "yes" with no explanation. It is the native speaker who requests an explanation (line 5) and, having received one (line 6), recasts the non-native speaker's explanation (lines 7 and 9) in a paraphrase of his response in line 6. The non-native speaker offers little support (a confirmatory repetition of his excuse in lines 8 and 10). Although this segment provides opportunities for the non-native speaker to elaborate on his excuse or to add an apology, and although the non-native speaker seems to recognize that a contribution is called for, he limits his contribution to the single-word repetitions produced in lines 8 and 10. The native speaker supports him, interpreting the minimal response in line 8 and adopting an appropriate attitude towards it (line 9, "oh no he has a headache").

Thus, rather than a situation in which the non-native speaker produces a full-blown one-turn refusal, in this exchange the native speaker and non-native speaker work out the non-native speaker's

excuse together, with the native speaker asking questions and react-
ing to the information provided, while the non-native speaker gives
minimal answers and confirms the native speaker's restatements.

5.2.2. Request for clarification

On the other hand, some non-native speakers formulated their own
requests for clarification, as in Example (7).

(7) Request for information/clarification (skydiving)

→   NNS: what is
        NS: what is skydiving

In this example the non-native speaker has just been informed
that she will be going skydiving with the host family that day; she
requests an explanation of the term *skydiving* ("what is").[17]

Thus, non-native speakers in these open role plays often spend
some of their time ostensibly in the negotiation of meaning, with
confirmations and requests for information. It should be kept in
mind, however, that the first interpretation — that the non-native
speaker is simply negotiating meaning — may not adequately represent what is going on, and that these acts may involve social as well
as linguistic moves. Thus, for instance, a commonly reported function of questions and clarification requests in refusal sequences is
verbal avoidance, as discussed by Bardovi-Harlig and Hartford
(1990), or putting off, as proposed by Labov and Fanshel (1977).

5.2.3. Agreement

A third response type that differed from responses in most previous
studies of refusals is agreement. While Beebe, Takahashi, and
Uliss-Weltz (1990), Imai (1981), Rubin (1983), and Ueda (1972)
mention general, vague, or unenthusiastic acceptance as types of refusals, sincere acceptances that evolve from initial refusals are not
discussed.

In several of the role plays, when faced with a persistent native speaker, the non-native speaker abandoned the attempt to refuse and finally accepted.   In Example (8), the non-native speaker's host mother at the weekend home-stay has offered to give the non-native speaker a punk-style haircut like her children's.   Agreement occurs after the non-native speaker has given two explicit refusals (lines 2 and 4) and a reason (line 6, only his barber, who is a hair specialist, can cut his hair):

(8) Agreement (haircut)

      1   NS: ok? and and I can cut your hair the same way.

→   2   NNS: ah oh no thank you

      3   NS: yes I'm I'm very good you see? you see what I've done with my children's hair?

               [[

→   4   NNS: but   but but n-n-n-n-n-n-no but but my hair was (my hair)

                                     [

      5   NS: it must be very hot it's summertime and (.) a lot of hair I mean

→   6   NNS: wait wait my my hair is uu always uhh spe special(ist) barber

      7   NS: oh ok

      8   NNS: so other people cannot ((nervous laugh)) my hair cut

      9   NS: why not I don't understand

   10 NNS: ummmm ((laugh)) I like this barber

   11 NS: uh huh

   12 NNS: yeah

   13 NS: but but you like my children's haircuts, right?

   14 NNS: ummm

   15 NS: so I c'n I can cut your hair and you can feel comfortable and cool?

→ 16 NNS: yeah please

In line 16, the non-native speaker abruptly changes his stance and agrees to let the native speaker cut his hair.   When asked afterwards if they would really have agreed to having their hair cut, almost half the non-native speakers polled said that they would, because she was their host mother.

Thus, the use of open role plays resulted in data which included three types of refuser contributions not normally discussed in analyses of discourse completion test data: 1) confirmations, 2) requests for information, and 3) sincere acceptances that evolved out of initial refusals.

6. Analysis of nonverbal aspects — Effect of video

So far we have been focusing primarily on the linguistic characteristics of refusals. However, understanding a full speech event entails having access to the full event. This includes access not only to the linguistic portion of a negotiated refusal, but to visual information as well. There are many aspects of a communicative event that are expressed, enhanced, or modified by nonverbal information. What we argue is the potential importance of nonverbal information (and hence of video) as a complement to studies on the production and comprehension of linguistic forms (e.g., vocabulary, grammar) and functions (e.g., speech acts).

In general, we have found four areas in which access to nonverbal information affected the interpretation of our data:

1. performance of nonverbal "speech" acts
2. aspects of the physical context that provide important information in interpreting the interaction
3. direction of gaze
4. expression of affect through posture, facial expressions, and gestures

These four areas will be discussed in some detail in the next sections, followed by a look at some of the problems associated with collecting and using videotaped data.

6.1. *Nonverbal messages*

In addition to those responses in which the non-native speaker used, if not propositions, at least lexical items from which a reasonable proposition could be inferred, non-native speakers sent real messages such as agreement or disagreement, deictic information, or even requests for information through nonverbal signals. Nonverbal resources were often used to confirm a native speaker statement or to request clarification or information. We contend that these nonverbal signs often performed the same functions as turns with recoverable propositions. (This will be discussed in greater detail in Chapter Four.)

Our transcripts contain a number of non-native speaker nonverbal signals, such as the nod in Example (9) and raised eyebrows in Example (10), which clearly carry intended communicative content. In these cases, the signals can function by themselves as a turn, performing an interactive function. (In the following example HS refers to a head shake, turning the head from side to side. Only non-native speaker nods and head shakes are included.)

(9) Nonverbal message: Confirmation (skydiving)
     (The non-native speaker is being invited to go skydiving.)

```
1   NNS: I'm afraid
         HS--------
2   NS:  she's afraid
3   NNS: mm
         NODS
4   NS:  oh no we have reservations for today
5   NNS: ohh I'm sorry ((laughs)) I'm afraid
6   NS:  you are
7   NNS: (yes) I'm (try to driving) NODS
         NODS
```

```
 8   NS:   you'd like to drive
                        [
 9   NNS:              today
                       NODS
10   NS:   oh you would like to take a drive
11   NNS: mm
12   NS:   but you're sure you don't want to go skydiving
13   NNS: NODS
```
→

In line 1, the non-native speaker expresses a fear of skydiving. The native speaker repeats the non-native speaker's statement to others in the role play, and the non-native speaker confirms this repetition with an *mm* accompanied by nods in line 3. After some discussion, the native speaker returns to the non-native speaker's fear (line 12), stating an implication (actually, an implicature) of this fear, that is, that the non-native speaker does not wish to skydive, as a request for confirmation. The non-native speaker confirms the native speaker's understanding with a (nonverbal) nod (line 13). Thus, in line 13 the nod signals confirmation.

In Example (10), as in Example (9), the native speaker attempts a restatement of the non-native speaker's previous statement, but in this case she seems to misinterpret the non-native speaker's meaning.

(10) Nonverbal message: Request for information/clarification (speech at church)
(As the host family and the non-native speaker prepare to go to church, the non-native speaker is informed that she has been requested to give a talk about herself at church.)

```
 1   NS:   ...they want you to give a speech to everybody in
            the church. is that ok?
 2   NNS: um um it's it's very short time for (me)
 3   NS:   oh ok you do not want to give a long speech
 4   NNS: ((raises eyebrows))
 5   NS:   you do not want to speak for a long time.
```
→

In this interaction, the non-native speaker utterance in line 2 ("it's it's very short time for (me)") can be interpreted to mean that she would not have enough time to prepare a speech. However, the native speaker indicates that she understands the non-native speaker to be saying that she is willing to give a speech if it is a short one (line 3). Thus, the native speaker's paraphrase does not necessarily correspond to the non-native speaker's meaning. Following line 3, the non-native speaker has an opportunity to confirm or disconfirm the native speaker's interpretation. Her raised eyebrows (line 4) convey her uncertainty and function as a question/request for further clarification (to which the native speaker responds, albeit perhaps inappropriately, with a reformulation of her paraphrase [line 5]).

The acts in Examples (9) and (10) represent aspects of negotiation of meaning which are missed when no record of nonverbal behaviors is kept.

6.2. *Physical context*

A second area in which videotaped data provided valuable information was in affording a physical context for the speech event. This is important because it serves to stabilize the context. An analogy can be made to reading a book. Where there are no visual cues, each individual reader is free to visualize in his/her own mind what the context is like. For reading, that might be positive; for speech act research, we contend that this is not a positive factor — especially as interlocutors may refer to or incorporate their awareness of physical events taking place in the interaction without explicitly mentioning these events, as in Example (11).

(11) Physical context: Native speaker withdrawing of hand
    (pierced ears)

    1   NS: are you absolutely sure? you you've definitely
                decided. I c'n call my girlfriend ((reaches for
                [imaginary] phone))

2   NNS: no ((laugh))
             HEAD SHAKE
             HAND WAVE-
→   3   NS: ((withdraws hand from phone))
     4   NNS: thank you
             NODS----

In this example the native speaker reaches for the phone as she makes her offer (line 1). In line 2, the non-native speaker refuses the offer. At this point, the native speaker withdraws her hand (line 3), and in line 4 the non-native speaker thanks her. Without the non-verbal information, the text would read like that in Example (12).

(12) Physical context: Native speaker withdrawal of hand omitted (pierced ears)

NS: are you absolutely sure? you you've definitely
       decided? I c'n call my girlfriend
NNS: no ((laugh)) thank you

The fact that the non-native speaker's "thank you" follows the native speaker's acceptance of the refusal, as indicated by her withdrawing of her hand from the telephone, is lost, along with the possible interpretation that the non-native speaker's "thank you" is at least partially prompted by the action. A (probably erroneous) interpretation that the non-native speaker was refusing (i.e., by saying "no thank you") could easily result from this version.

6.3. *Directionality and intensity of attention*

A third advantage of the videotaped record was that we could see the direction and to some extent the intensity of the interactants' attention. We were thus able to observe apparent discomfort, and in the role plays we could see when interlocutors were going off line (e.g., looking at notes, gesturing or commenting off camera). The intensity with which a non-native speaker, for example, focused on a native speaker interlocutor in attempting to understand the native speaker could also be observed, as in the following example. (To facilitate reader interpretation, all of the nonverbal gestures and posture are represented with capital letters in the following example).

(13) Non-native speaker intensity of attention (pierced ears)

```
        1    NS:    ((laughs)) do ya think it's terrible?
        2    NNS:   yeh ((laughs))
                    HEAD SHAKE
        3    NS:    ahh, (.) y'sure? I- y'know what?=
                                    [
→       4    NNS:                        LEANS FORWARD
        5    NS:    =see- see the way I have my ears pierced
                    HAND TO EAR---------------------------
                    [
→       6    NNS:   LEANING FORWARD-------------------
        7    NS:    doesn't that look cool?
→       8    NNS:   LEANS FURTHER, PEERS, HAND TO
                    OWN EAR
        9    NS:    see the way I have my ears pierced?
                    remember I've got four=
        10   NNS:   =um=
→                   LEANING FORWARD
        11   NS:    =I've got four holes here in this ear?
        12   NNS:   yeh
```

In this example, the non-native speaker's attention is on the native speaker throughout the interaction (lines 4, 6, 8, 10). As the native speaker shows her ears with the (imaginary) four holes (line 5), the non-native speaker leans forward and peers intently (lines 6 and 8), continuing to lean toward the native speaker as she remarks on the four holes in her ear. The non-native speaker's focused attention on the native speaker's message serves as an external reflection of his work at comprehending that message. (See Chapter Five for a visual representation of the non-native speaker's posture.)

6.4. *Affect*

A fourth advantage in having videotaped data in addition to oral data was that we were able to observe that even in role plays, nonverbal information aided not only in the negotiation of meaning, but in the negotiation of affect (this will be dealt with in greater detail in Chapter Five), a concept that is particularly important when dealing with face-threatening acts. This aspect of interaction is often carried out through vocal characteristics such as intonation, pitch, and voice setting, but may also rely on facial expressions, head movements, gestures, and posture. The contrast was especially noticeable in a comparison of three of the ear piercing situations (discussed at length in Chapter Five).

In one case, the non-native speaker remains practically immobile, with her hands behind her back, smiling during the entire interaction. The other speakers use body posture (e.g., leaning), nods and head shakes, arm and hand gestures, as well as facial expressions and head positions (e.g., turned away) which convey attention, express attitudes of agreement and disagreement, and in some instances modify the verbal message. The non-native speaker in Example (13) above focused closely on the native speaker; later on in the interaction, his responses were underlined by broad, dramatic use of his hands and arms, which communicated the intensity of his refusal.

(14) Non-native speaker gestures emphasizing intensity of refusal
     (pierced ears)

> NS: I mean have you really thought about it? You're sure
>   you don't want to?
> NNS: no I don't want
>   ARM OUTSTRETCHED

Text alone is often inadequate to represent the intensity of the message. And even a transcript with gestures indicated does not communicate the full impression. (See Chapter Five for a visual representation of the non-native speaker's gesture in the previous example.)

In general, the impressions conveyed by different individuals may vary greatly, even when their language is comparable. It is only through the use of video that we have access to the full range of affect expressed by speakers.

6.5. *Disadvantages*

We have pointed out the many ways that videotaped data have enriched our understanding of the communicative event we were investigating, in this case communication between individuals who did not fully share a language code. However, there are clearly disadvantages which we point out here: 1) video equipment is cumbersome to use in data collection; at least with adults, it can be used only in planned and perhaps contrived instances, as with role plays, 2) gathering data with video is more intrusive than gathering data with audio-recorders only, 3) some subjects who do not mind being audio-taped do mind being videotaped; in cases in which researchers are dealing with different cultures, with different understandings of the value of research or different attitudes toward appearing on video, video-taping may be particularly problematic, 4) showing videotaped data may result in viewers being distracted by the physical appearance of the participants rather than focusing on the communication event that they are engaged in, 5) videotaped data are unusually difficult to transcribe. It is a challenge to bring alive nonverbal information when all one has are the confines of the printed page. Furthermore, merely having access to the full speech event does not mean that all of the information can be extracted and transcribed. One always has to pick and choose what one will use. If a participant moves one foot, does one transcribe it? If a participant moves one hand, does one transcribe it? If a participant shrugs one shoulder, does one transcribe it? In other words, where does one draw the limits? Close observation is needed to determine what is significant to the interaction and what is not.

Thus, in face-to-face interactions, non-native speakers may call on a number of resources in negotiating refusals. And they may employ these resources to convey different meanings, depending on the context. The availability of video has opened the door to the possibility of capturing information that not only complements the linguistic data available through tape recording, but in some cases forces us to reinterpret those data (as in the case of nonverbal messages) or to reconsider them as perhaps representing only one (albeit basic) message feature available to and affecting interactants within a larger context (as in the case of nonverbal behavior conveying affective information). The challenge is to use this access to nonverbal information together with linguistic data to understand how non-native speakers use the resources at their disposal in face-to-face interaction.

7. Conclusion

To summarize, the use of videotaped open role plays results in a wealth of information about how non-native speakers, in the case of the data presented in this book, non-native speakers with relatively low levels of proficiency, may work their way through a refusal with a native speaker.

The choice of an open role play, which allows non-native speakers to work with an interactant toward an outcome, illustrated that refusals often require a number of turns to effect a response. The number of turns required may reflect the natural and common need for conversationalists to interact to solve a problem, for example, through negotiation and elaboration of meaning. A greater number of turns may be necessary when a non-native speaker is involved than when only native speakers are conversing. For instance, a non-native speaker may also need to try out more ploys to resolve disharmony (see Bardovi-Harlig and Hartford 1990). Or, the number of turns may indicate the persistence or stubbornness of the individual native speaker interlocutor and the non-native speaker respondent.

In addition, the use of open role plays has shown that the performance of acts such as refusals involves the use of resources that are not required or even appropriate in noninteractional role play. Thus, it is through a more open elicitation format that we were able to identify three acts — confirmation, request for clarification, and agreement — which occurred with some frequency and which have not been identified in most previous work on refusals (but see Bardovi-Harlig and Hartford 1991; Morrow 1995; Turnbull 1993, 1994).

These classes of acts are special in that, unlike the acts conventionally associated with refusals, they are characteristic of dynamic interaction in general. Their occurrence in stressful negotiations is especially appropriate and plays a crucial role in the non-native speaker's negotiation of a response. These three classes are particularly effective because in addition to their obvious speech act function, individual instances of the acts can represent a discourse tactic or social maneuver designed to soften the unpleasantness of a refusal. For instance, a refusal that develops into a series of non-native speaker confirmations (as in Example 6) may allow the non-native speaker to build up solidarity with the native speaker in a face-threatening situation. Or a request for information or clarification may function as an avoidance tactic or a put-off. And the fact that a change of heart occasionally took place after an initial refusal, and agreement ultimately occurred, represents the ultimate in refusal alleviation.

Thus, as soon as we consider a refusal not as a simple response to a static situation but as a dynamic negotiated achievement, it becomes clear that the inclusion of confirmations, requests for clarification and agreements in any discussion of possible refusal responses is indicated.

A second practical methodological implication resulted from our use of videotapes, which enabled us to capture important nonverbal aspects of the interaction such as the performance of meaningful interactional acts, relevant characteristics of the situation, direction of speaker gaze, and expressions of affect.

Our data have revealed the existence of a richer variety of meaningful resources and maneuvers than has generally been documented in discussions of non-native refusals. The negotiations we have described go far beyond the notion of a simple response consisting of linguistically analyzable units. Rather, the responses involve an interaction not only between what the non-native speaker wants to say and what her interlocutor wants her to say, but how to say it — what grammar, non-verbal and discourse tactics to use to carry out both her social obligations and her personal wishes effectively in a particular situation.

While we recognize that important work has been done collecting data on the selection and realization of linguistic acts across cultures using written discourse completion tests and closed role plays, the addition of videotaped interactional data from open role plays can only enrich our understanding of speech acts. In the following chapters, we provide additional detailed analyses of our data; these analyses crucially depend on an understanding of a full and complete picture of a refusal sequence along with accompanying nonverbal information.

Chapter 3
Episodes

1. Introduction

In the previous chapters, we have looked at general characteristics of refusals (and refusal interactions) in English and the effects of data collection techniques on the results of speech act research. In this and succeeding chapters, we move to consideration of particular instances of refusals and the insights they suggest concerning the work done by non-native speakers and native speakers involved in face-threatening interactions.

As has been noted by many scholars, in conversations involving non-native speakers, there is often a lack of shared assumptions and shared background. The consequences of this lack of common background are at times particularly acute. Gumperz and Tannen (1979) have in fact argued that cross-cultural communication is precisely where one can see most clearly how conversation can go awry. In cross-cultural conversations, interlocutors often have to work harder to convey and understand meaning and intention, to establish appropriate social relationships, and, in situations requiring resolution, to reach a mutually satisfying outcome. Cross-cultural interactions may require more time and may involve more inferencing problems than similar interactions between conversationalists from the same culture. By investigating the characteristics of conversations (e.g., how conversations are structured, how outcomes are negotiated) which fall outside the so-called norm, researchers can gain insights into the resources available to the participants and the conversational norms to which each participant is orienting.

This chapter has two parts. First, we argue for a unit of analysis, which we call an *episode*, an analytical unit that we find necessary to an understanding of the complexity of refusals. To illustrate the use of episodes, we refer to one long refusal sequence as a way of demonstrating a phenomenon (a series of refusals) that occurred throughout our data. Second, we analyze this sequence using episodes as a basis for understanding the complexities inherent in refusal sequences and as a basis for understanding the evolution from initial non-native speaker refusal to native speaker nonacceptance of that refusal and finally to reluctant acceptance of the refusal by the native speaker.

2. The episode

In analyzing our data, we found that the units of analysis discussed in work on second language speech acts do not adequately capture the richness of non-native refusals. To define and delimit the stretch of discourse directly involved in refusing, we propose that refusal responses can profitably be analyzed in terms of episodes.

Episodes have been discussed elsewhere in the discourse analysis literature. van Dijk (1982) in his investigation of episodes as semantic units characterizes them as "coherent sequences of sentences of a discourse, linguistically marked for beginning and/or end, and further defined in terms of some kind of 'thematic unity'..." (p. 177). He later goes on to provide the following characteristics of episodes:

1. an episode is conceived of as part of a whole
2. the parts and the whole involve sequences of events or actions
3. the episode should be unified and have some relative independence

As noted, van Dijk's is essentially a semantic notion. However, he also claims that episodes are psychologically relevant units.

The notion of episode that we utilize in this chapter is both similar to and different from van Dijk's episode.[18] It is similar in at least two ways: First, there is a discernible beginning and an end, and second, episodes are relatively independent, that is, each can stand alone as, in this case, a request/refusal sequence. However, we are dealing with an episode within the domain of a speech act. Hence, the notion of sequence of events or actions is largely irrelevant. Further, we are not making any claims at this point for psychological relevance of the unit of episode within a speech act.

There are two parts to our definition of episode:

1. An episode is bounded on one side by an eliciting act (in this case, a request) and on the other by either dialogue not directly related to the eliciting act or a recycling of the eliciting act.
2. An episode must include some kind of response (e.g., in the form of a perceived refusal or acceptance) directed at or relevant to the opening eliciting act. So, for example, a request which is ignored (for whatever reason) does not constitute an eliciting move in an episode.

Thus, all the talk within an episode pertains to the negotiation of a response to an eliciting act.

Example (15) illustrates one episode in a series. In this example, the non-native speaker, a male in his late 20s, is a guest in the home of a native speaker. The host family has gone to a neighbor's house and has given specific instructions to the non-native speaker not to let anyone in the house. While the native speaker is out, a woman claiming to be the host's cousin has appeared at the door and has asked if she can come in and wait until Quentin, her cousin (and the host father), comes home. The non-native speaker has refused, and the native speaker is recycling the request for the third time. (The vertical line | marks the beginning of an eliciting act — here, a request.)

(15) Episode 3 (cousin)

→　　NS:　　| oh come on
　　　NNS:　 yeah
→　　NS:　　just let me in
　　　NNS:　 yeah uh
→　　NS:　　just yeh let me in
　　　NNS:　 yeah oh so ah I think you had better to go neighbor's house to uh to meet him
　　　NS:　　oh Quentin oh wh wh what neighbor's house is he at boy he's not going to hear the last of this
　　　　　　　　　　　　[
　　　NNS:　　　　　　　　　excuse excuse me I don't know
　　　NS:　　you don't know whe-
　　　NNS:　 yeah

```
NS:    aiiii
NNS:   but not so far from (here) maybe I
       (near the house)
         [
NS:    so what am I supposed to do drive around?  I
       don't know his neighbors either
NNS:   uh y- you can uh go by walk
NS:    thank you thank you very much very kind of=
             [        [          [
NNS:         yeah     yeah       yeah
NS:    =you I've driven f- 13 hours and I can walk around in
       the neighborhood and y- I don't know where I'm
       looking I don't know who t- whose house to go to?=
                                      [
NNS:                                  but
NS:    =| come on come on just let me in let me in=
```

This episode begins with an eliciting act (request) when the native speaker says "oh come on," "just let me in," "just yeh let me in." It ends when she repeats the request in the last line "come on come on just let me in let me in." This is where a new episode begins. All the talk here within an episode pertains to the eliciting act and negotiation of a response to it.

Episodes can also terminate with dialogue or action not directly related to resolving a request. This kind of termination of an episode occurs frequently after an outcome has been reached. This is exemplified in Example (16). Here, the native speaker asks for the fifth time to be allowed to enter.

(16) Episode 5 (cousin)

```
→   1    NS:   | let me in an n let me sit uh come in and sit
                 down and wait
    2    NNS:  but I can't decide uh you come in (.) I I can't
                 do that uh I can't what I do this situation (I
                 can't do)
    3    NS:   ((sighs)) ah huh huh I don't believe it ok
```

→   all right ok all right when ya when ya tell
when you see Quentin tell him he's a son of a
gun ok
((NS leaves))

In line 3, the native speaker finally accepts the non-native speaker's refusal to admit her to her cousin's house and moves on to bid farewell, with a parting shot at Quentin, her cousin.

3. A complete refusal sequence

In Example (17), we show how a single refusal-response sequence is played out in its entirety — in this case, five episodes, the boundaries of which are indicated by the thick horizontal lines. These lines mark the end of one episode as well as the beginning of another. In some cases, there may be intervening material which links the two episodes. This material bridges the episodes and may be part of the same turn as the subsequent request. In other words, one episode does not always follow directly on the heels of another. The bridge material is sandwiched in between and lends a sense of coherence to the discourse.

In Example (17) we see that within each episode lengthy discussions often occur in which each person negotiates his/her way through towards a final resolution. In the first four episodes, the attempted resolutions are not accepted by both parties. Specifically, the native speaker's lack of acceptance of the non-native speaker's attempts to refuse results in the recycling of the initial request.

(17) Complete sequence with 5 episodes (cousin)

     NS: oh hi how are you doing
     NNS: oh fine thank you
               [
     NS: is uh is uh Quentin in
     NNS: no uh no I'm not

NS: no he's not in

       [

NNS: uh no no he's not in

NS: ahh where'd he go

NNS: ahh he goes to neighbor (house)

            [

Reason for Request	NS:	ah well do you mind if- I'm I'm his cousin and I'm just passing through Lansing tonight
	NNS:	mm
	NS:	and I'm I'm on my way to Detroit I'm on a on a business trip
	NNS:	mm
	NS:	and and uh I'd like to see him I've got about

Episode→ 1		half an hour or so | would you mind if I come in and wait for a minute or so an a til he comes back
	NNS:	ah no wait wait I'm a guest to uh this home the- I can't uh I don't uh uh um I can't I don't know what uh I do this situation then ah
	NS:	I'm sorry?
	NNS:	uh he he don't tell me uh
	NS:	ahh
	NNS:	if another person come in his home
	NS:	yeah yeah but I I I'm his cousin I'm sure it's going to be ok=
		[
	NNS:	but
	NNS:	=((laughs)) I don't know=
	NS:	=I I know it'll be all right=
	NNS:	=my first time to meet you (.) I don't know you
	NS:	y'know actually this is the first time I've

```
          met you too how do you do=
                [
NNS:              wait wait
NS:        =nice to meet you
           [
NNS:    I think uh I
           think uh he came back uh not so late
           ((slightly louder))uh huh yeh uh please wait
           uh your car
NS:        ((gasps))
NNS:    ((slightly louder)) uh uh if you want to meet
           uh
NS:        I can't believe this
                    [
NNS:              him
NS:        I can't believe this this is my cousin this is my
           cousin
           [
NNS:    but I don't know you
                [
NS:                    we grew up together we went
           fishing together
NNS:    uh
NS:        you mean to tell me I can't even come in his
           house
NNS:    (but) I don't know you are cousin I don't
           know
NS:        well who uh a- a- a- a- a- uh- uh- that's not
           my problem
NNS:    oh yeah
NS:        that's not my problem you don't know? what
           do you what are you talking about this is=
           [
NNS:    nn
NS:        = Quentin's my cousin what are you doing
NNS:    oohnn
```

NS: you're not going to let me in his house=

                                            [

NNS: uhh

NS: =I can't believe this

       [[

NNS: I   said   it's my business I now
       I homestay yeh I cannot door open

                              [

NS: what do you mean it's your
       business who are you how do I know you're
       not a burglar

NNS: no

Bridging   NS: I'm a oh boy boy Quentin's not going to hear
Material

Episode→   the last of this |come on let me in
   2   NNS: aoo
               NS: come on I've been traveling all the way from
                      Muskegon
               NNS: oh yeah

                              [

               NS: and I was win in Chi- Chicago the night
                      before I'm beat let me in let me sit down and
                      wait for Quentin this is ridiculous

                              [[

               NNS: ahh   so
                      I feel very sorry yeah but I so I cannot decide
                      this door open

Episode→   NS: |oh come on
   3   NNS: yeah
               NS: just let me in
               NNS: yeah uh

NS: just yeh let me in

NNS: yeah ah so uh I think you had better to go
       neighbor's house to uh to meet him

NS: oh Quentin oh wh wh what neighbor's house
       is he at boy he's not
        going to hear the last of this
       [

NNS: excuse excuse me I don't know

NS: you don't know whe-

NNS: yeah

NS: aiiii

NNS: but not so far from (here) maybe I
       (near the house)
       [

NS: so what am I supposed to do drive around? I
       don't know his neighbors either

NNS: uh y- you can uh go by walk

NS: thank you thank you very much very kind of=
                    [[[

NNS: yeah   yeah   yeah

NS: =you

Bridging   NS: I've driven f- 13 hours and I can walk around
Material   in the neighborhood and y- I don't know
                       where I'm looking I don't know who t-whose
                        house to go to
                       [

                NNS: but

Episode→   NS: | come on come on just let
4   me in let me in let me sit down and=
                          [

                NNS: ahhh

                NS: =take it easy and rest for a while I'm thirsty
                                             [

                NNS: ahm

```
              yeah
    NS:       yeah
    NNS:      it's a problem
    NS:       yeah it's a problem
    NNS:      uh it's a problem
```

Bridging   NS: I'm tired I'm beat
Material   NNS: umm yeah

Episode→   NS: |let me in an n let me sit uh come in and
   5   sit down and wait
             NNS: but I can't decide uh you come in (.) I I can't
                    do that uh uh I can't what I do this situation (I
                    can't do)
             NS: ((sighs)) ah huh huh I don't believe it ok all
                    right ok all right when ya when ya tell when
                    you see Quentin tell him he's a son of a gun
                    ok
                  ((NS leaves))

It is evident from these data that any characterization of refusals as simply a chain of repeated requests would not be adequate. Rather, what we have are multiple episodes, each of which takes on a character of its own. For example, the first episode begins cordially with some hedging and expression of confusion by the non-native speaker ("I don't know what uh I do this situation") and ends with anger on the part of the native speaker ("I can't believe this") and determination on the part of the non-native speaker ("I cannot door open"). The second episode has little evidence of cordiality, but does indicate resolve by the non-native speaker with the inclusion of the word *decide* ("I cannot decide this door open"). Episode 4 takes on a plaintive quality as the native speaker once again requests "...come on come on just let me in let me in," and the non-native speaker begins to show sympathy toward her plight. A summary of the linguistic features of the entire interaction fails to capture the complexity evidenced in this refusal. A more apt way of describing such refusals is by means of a spiral in which participant intentions and relationships evolve at each step, with each response potentially affected by what has come before.

The interaction is particularly long because it is a played out event, a fact which poses problems for describing and comparing our results with data from non-interactive data collection instruments such as discourse completion tests, notebook data, and oral responses to taped elicitations. The episode defines a segment in a larger refusal sequence that is loosely comparable to these single elicitation measures.

The episode also offers the researcher a means of comparing sometimes lengthy negotiations across recycled speech acts. One obvious factor contributing to the length of the interaction in this transcript, for example, is the persistence of the native speaker and the recalcitrance of the non-native speaker. Whereas in some of the data we collected, as mentioned in Chapter Two, non-native speakers gave in and accepted the native speaker's request/offer/ suggestion/invitation after one or two attempts to refuse, certain situations, such as a stranger requesting admittance to the host family's home, were never accepted (see Chapter Six for a discussion). The episode provides a unit for comparing various types of data and the complexity necessary for resolution.

The episode can also provide insight into the development of non-native speaker linguistic responses across turns. It has been noted that a non-native speaker often needs time to formulate ideas and express them with an appropriate degree of explicitness. In our transcript, at first the non-native speaker appears to be somewhat confused by the native speaker's response to his reasons for refusing. However, as the interaction progresses, the non-native speaker demonstrates greater resolve until he finally responds to the request in Episode 2 with a gracious but firm "very sorry yeah but I so I cannot decide this door open." Thus, it may be that the length of this interaction is partly due to the longer time it takes a non-native speaker to arrive at a point at which a native speaker might have arrived in a brief time. And it is the native speaker's recycling of her request (i.e., the initiation of Episode 2) which provides the opportunity for the non-native speaker to pull this response together.

In addition, the series of episodes provides the researcher with sequential units that can be used to examine the non-native speaker's developing approach to the refusal. It has been noted that because even advanced non-native speakers are not familiar with many cultural and linguistic norms, they often try out a variety of (sometimes contradictory) means to see what works (cf. Bardovi-Harlig and Hartford 1991). This is reflected in our transcript by the non-native speaker's shifts in his approach to the refusal — from polite to adamant (in Episode 1) to helpful (as in the counterproposal in Episode 3) to empathetic (in Episode 4) — some of which are represented by semantic formulas that are not as common in English data (e.g., counterproposals and empathy). The comparison of episodes within the same sequence enables the researcher to consider the evolution of the non-native speaker's responses across the text, with each episode representing a fresh opportunity to trot out new approaches or reformulate old ones and see how they play out.

Thus, we have posited and defined a unit of analysis which we have called an episode. As we noted, the talk within an episode relates to the negotiation of a response to an eliciting act, with bridging material often used to move coherently from one episode to another. By examining episodes as self-contained units that build on one another, we are able to gain a clearer picture of the evolution of participant responses across multiple turns and recycled speech acts.

In the next section, we make use of the episode to analyze in more detail the semantic formulas employed by the non-native speaker in the extended interaction presented above.

4. Analysis

As mentioned in Chapter One, Beebe, Takahashi, and Uliss-Weltz (1990) analyzed the refusals in their data in terms of the frequency, sequencing, and content of the semantic formulas used in a single response to a single elicitation, noting differences that reflected the L1 background of the speaker. What we argue on the basis of the data given in earlier sections of this chapter is that in an extended interaction, there may be a recycling of requests and responses which involves more than either a simple chain of repeated requests and responses (cf. Labov and Fanshel 1977) or a straightforward transfer of L1 semantic formulas into the second language by the refuser (cf. Beebe, Takahashi, and Uliss-Weltz 1990). Rather, the non-native speaker's choice of semantic formula and content evolves across episodes, revealing a set of resources for accommodating to and possibly learning from a new situation.[19] In other words, descriptions of refusal responses in terms of the semantic formulas used in a single turn provide only a partial picture of the interaction.

Using the notion of episode, we now analyze the interaction depicted above, considering not only 1) the formulas the non-native speaker used and 2) their content, but also 3) their distribution across the interaction. The results indicate that while the semantic formulas and content used in the interaction correspond closely to those found by Beebe, Takahashi, and Uliss-Weltz, it is also informative to provide an account of the distribution of these formulas and their content within an interaction, as such an account can provide a look at the development of refusal resources across turns and episodes.

4.1. *Quantitative analysis*

Using Beebe, Takahashi, and Uliss-Weltz's classification system, we determined that the non-native speaker employed the following semantic formulas in this series of refusal episodes:

Table 2. Frequency of semantic formulas in Cousin

Semantic Formulas	Frequency
Direct	
"no"	1
expression of inability	1
Reason (explanation)	5
	(10 tokens)
Statement of regret	1
Alternative	2

The data also included two explicit expressions of empathy, which we suggest function in this instance as a semantic formula rather than what Beebe, Takahashi, and Uliss-Weltz refer to as an adjunct (see Chapter Two). We return to this point in section 4.2.1.5.

4.2. *Qualitative analysis*

More revealing than a quantitative description of the semantic formulas used in Example (17) is a consideration of the form and content and the sequencing of the semantic formulas in the text.

4.2.1. Form and content of the semantic formulas

The analysis in this section focuses on five semantic formulas: 1) direct refusals, 2) reasons, 3) statements of regret, 4) alternatives, and 5) expressions of empathy.

4.2.1.1. Direct refusal

As noted above, in the entire interaction, there is only one instance of a direct refusal: "no." This explicit refusal occurs in response to the native speaker's first request to enter. It is immediately followed in the same turn by two reasons.[20]

(18)   Direct refusal (cousin)

      NS: ...I come in and wait for a minute or so an a til he comes back

      NNS: ah no wait wait I'm a guest to uh this home the- I can't uh I don't uh uh um I can't I don't know what uh I do this situation then ah

In Labov and Fanshel's (1977) terms, this sequence constitutes an instance of a refusal with an account — a relatively direct, acceptable way of formulating a refusal.

    In addition, a negative expression of ability (also classified as a direct refusal by Beebe, Takahashi, and Uliss-Weltz) occurs in the expression of Reason (d) (see section 4.2.2). The non-native speaker explains that he has a responsibility to his host and follows this explanation with the negative statement of ability "I cannot door open."

4.2.1.2. Reason

In contrast with the single occurrence of a direct refusal, five slightly different reasons are ultimately put forward during the interaction. An examination of the content of these reasons reveals that they are all related to the non-native speaker's status as a guest in the house and to the implications which he indicates are inherent in that status. We have characterized the content of these reasons as:

a. non-native speaker's status as guest
b. non-native speaker's ignorance of what to do[21]
c. non-native speaker's ignorance of native speaker, who claims to be the host's cousin
d. non-native speaker's responsibility to his host
e. non-native speaker's inability to decide what to do

As mentioned, each of these reasons is related to some aspect of the non-native speaker's current "role" as guest. Reason (a) defines that status, and Reasons (b), (c), and (e) emphasize the impotence (i.e., the ignorance and lack of power) associated with his role. Reason (d), on the other hand, focuses on a different aspect of the guest's status: the implied power in his (assumed) responsibility to represent his host's interests.

4.2.1.3. Regret

The single instance of an expression of regret cooccurs with Reason (e) ("...so I feel very sorry yeah but I so I cannot decide this door open").

4.2.1.4. Alternative

Two alternatives are proposed by the non-native speaker during the five episodes. The semantic content of these alternatives, both of which are treated as offensive and inappropriate by the native speaker cousin, is as follows:

1. Wait in the car
2. Look for the host in the neighborhood

Alternative 1 (wait in the car) represents a realistic suggestion if one accepts that the native speaker cousin is not going to be admitted. However, it is unclear whether this alternative was considered unacceptable 1) because it was proposed by the refuser (rather than by the petitioner), or 2) because of the apparent lack of thought for the native speaker's comfort that the content seems to indicate, or 3) because of the non-native speaker's choice of language ("Please wait your car if you want to meet him"), which includes no apology or statement of regret. This alternative is treated as unacceptable by the native speaker, who responds by gasping and then complaining "I can't believe this."

The second alternative, a suggestion that the cousin should go to the neighbor's house to find the host — even though the non-native speaker is unable to provide directions to the neighbor's house, may indeed be totally inappropriate (as it is undoubtedly taken to be by the native speaker, who responds with sarcasm). However, the content of the suggestion could result from unshared assumptions of the cousin's knowledge of Mr. Quentin's friends in the neighborhood.

In any case, both of the alternatives prove to be singularly ineffective. This is not always the case with proposed alternatives. In another role play of the same situation, a non-native speaker guest offered to accompany the native speaker cousin to find the host Mr. Quentin, as in Example (19).

(19) Successful alternative (cousin)

> NS: boy Mr. Quentin's going to be very unhappy when he realizes that he that his only cousin wasn't allowed in his home, that's very sad
>
> NNS: ahh ((laughs)) so please ((laughing)) uh please go to his neighbor's with me now
>
> NS: uh huh
>
> NNS: so uh m you c-can you will be able to see him and Mr. Mr. Wuin Quint Mr. Quentin uh uh will explain about um about me about me.
>
> NS: oh- ok all right
>
> NNS: so please go to him with me
>
> NS: ok all right so come on
>
> NS: uh hhuh
>
> NS: all right ok ok all right
>
> NNS: thank you

The role play ended with the native speaker's acceptance of the offer (i.e., a Final Outcome of a Nonaccept [Alternative]).

4.2.1.5. Empathy

The fifth proposed semantic formula, expression of empathy, comes in response to the native speaker's complaint of thirst and fatigue, acknowledging her situation (e.g., "It's a problem"). Expressions of empathy are treated by Beebe, Takahashi, and Uliss-Weltz as an adjunct to refusals rather than as a semantic formula. However, because of the strategic role that these verbal indications of empathy seem to play in this interaction, we propose that in this case they serve the function of refusal. That is, now that the refusal is well established, the non-native speaker's use of empathy indicates among other things that the refusal remains in effect, without specifically addressing the request. (Empathy under these conditions might be considered a type of avoidance.) Clearly, such a use of empathy would probably not occur in analyses in which only data from an initial refusal is considered.

4.2.2. Sequencing of Semantic Formulas

In the interaction under consideration in this chapter, the non-native speaker employs the major semantic formulas in Beebe, Takashi, and Uliss-Weltz's classification, albeit with differing success, often depending on the specific content of the semantic formula used. If we take the analysis one step further and consider the sequencing of formulas across the entire interaction (i.e., if we look at the distribution of refusal acts across episodes and interpret them in terms of how well they function to effect the non-native speaker's goal), we see the drawing on and discarding of a series of attitudes and the evolution of an approach which builds on knowledge of the prior use and effect of previously expressed responses.

We will consider the entire interaction, episode by episode. Episode 1 includes a greater number of different semantic formulas for refusal than any of the subsequent episodes. The non-native speaker guest initially responds to the native speaker cousin's request to enter the host's house with a turn rich in refusal indicators, beginning with a direct "no", followed by Reason (a) ("I'm a guest to this home") and then by Reason (b) ("I don't know what I do this situation"), which is closely related to Reason (a). In a sense, the non-native speaker opts for clarity in establishing his position from the outset. In the case of Reasons (a) and (b), he selects accounts that emphasize his lack of power and his confusion with respect to the situation. Episode 1 continues as, in response to the native speaker cousin's rejection of Reason (b), the non-native speaker guest goes on to articulate another aspect of his situation, his ignorance of the fact that the native speaker really is Quentin's cousin (Reason c), and to offer an alternative (Alternative 1, "Please wait your car"), neither of which is effective. Finally, he explicitly states (with increased intensity) a reason which is also a consequence of his status as a guest alone in his host's house: It is indeed his responsibility to refuse to admit someone he does not know ("It's my business").

In what follows we include in the left-hand margin our analysis of the semantic formulas used to perform the refusals, along with additional moves or social acts used by the participants to negotiate their way through this refusal sequence. The analysis will focus only on the non-native speaker's use of the refusal formulas discussed above, which are highlighted in boldface.

(20) Episode 1

REQUEST 1	NS:	|...would you mind if I come in and wait for a minute or so an a til he comes back
Direct "no" **Reason a** **Reason b**	NNS:	ah no wait wait I'm a guest to uh this home the- I can't uh I don't uh uh um I can't I don't know what uh I do this situation then eh
Request for Clarification	NS:	I'm sorry?
Clarification of Reason b	NNS:	uh he he don't tell me uh
	NS:	ahh
	NNS:	if another person come in his home
Rejection of Reason b	NS:	yeah yeah but I I I'm his cousin I'm sure it's going to be ok=
	NNS:	[but
Repetition of Reason b (or begin Reason c)		= ((laughs)) I don't know=
Repetition of Rejection of b	NS:	=I I know it'll be all right=
Reason c	NNS:	=my first time to meet you (.) I don't know you
Response to Reason c	NS:	y'know actually this is the first time I've met you too how do=
	NNS:	[wait wait
	NS:	=you do nice to meet you
Reason for Alter-	NNS:	[I think uh I

native 1

		think uh he came back uh not so late ((slightly louder)) uh huh yeh uh
Alternative 1 (Reaction) (=Reject Alternative 1)	NS:	please wait uh your car ((gasps))
	NNS:	((slightly louder)) uh uh if uh you want to meet uh
	NS:	I can't believe this
		[
	NNS:	him
(Reaction cont.) Reason for Reaction/ Rejection	NS:	I can't believe this this is my cousin this is my cousin
		[
Restatement of Reason c	NNS:	but I don't know you
		[
	NS:	we grew up together we went fishing together
	NNS:	uh
Statement of Refusal Implication	NS:	you mean to tell me I can't even come in his house
Restatement of Reason c+	NNS:	(but) I don't know you are cousin I don't know
Challenge (=Rejection of Reason c)	NS:	well who uh a- a- a- a- a- uh- uh- that's not my problem
	NNS:	oh yeah
(Rejection cont.)	NS:	that's not my problem you don't know? what do you=
		[
	NNS:	nn
	NS:	=what are you talking about
Reason for Rejection of c		this is Quentin's my cousin what are you doing
	NNS:	oohnn

Statement of Re-
fusal Implication
(Reaction)
	NS: you're not going to let me in=
	            [
	NNS: uhh
	NS: =his house I can't believe this
	         [[

Reason d	NNS: I said it's my business I now I home-
Negative Ability	stay yeh I cannot door open [
Challenge (=Rejection of Reason d) Denial	NS: what do you mean it's your business who are you how do I know you're not a burglar NNS: no

In Episode 2, the non-native speaker guest returns to a self-effacing approach (Reason e): He is unable to make the decision to admit the native speaker cousin. In fact, this is another way of looking at Reason (d), that he is responsible for deciding not to admit the cousin. However, by prefacing Reason (e) with his only expression of regret in the entire interaction, the contrast with the more assertive attitude he expressed with Reason (d) is emphasized.

(21) Episode 2

REQUEST 2	NS: |come on let me in NNS: aoo
Reason for Request	NS: come on I've been traveling all the way from Muskegon NNS: oh yeah [
	NS: and I was win in Chi- Chicago
Repetition of Request	the night before I'm beat let me in let me sit down and wait for Quentin this is ridiculous [[NNS: ahh so

| **Regret** | I feel very sorry yeah but I so I |
| **Reason e** | cannot decide this door open |

In Episode 3, the non-native speaker proposes a second alternative — that the native speaker cousin try to find the neighbor's house that Quentin is visiting — a suggestion that is greeted with sarcasm by the native speaker cousin. Although the sarcasm is apparently unrecognized by the non-native speaker, he seems to realize that this proposal is also unsuccessful and possibly inappropriate.

(22) Episode 3

REQUEST 3	NS:	|oh come on
	NNS:	yeah
	NS:	just let me in
	NNS:	yeah uh
	NS:	just yeh let me in
Alternative 2	NNS:	yeah ah so uh I think you had better to go neighbor's house to uh to meet him
Request for Clarification re Alternative 2/ Complaint	NS:	oh Quentin oh uh wh What neighbor's house is he at boy he's not going to hear the last of this [
Apology Response to Request for Clarification	NNS:	excuse excuse me I don't know
Request for Confirmation	NS:	you don't know whe-
Confirmation	NNS:	yeah
(Reaction)	NS:	aiiii
Elaboration of Response to Req for Confirmation	NNS:	but not so far from (here) maybe I (near the house) [
(Sarcastic) Request for Clarification Reason for Request	NS:	so what am I supposed to do drive around? I don't know his neighbors either

for Clarification (Sincere)	NNS:	uh y-you can uh go by walk
Response to Req for Clarification (Sarcastic)	NS:	thank you thank you very much=
Thanks (Sincere)	NNS:	[[yeah yeah
Acknowledgment	NS:	=very kind of you
	NNS:	[yeah

In Episode 4, the non-native speaker neither attempts to explain his refusal nor offers an alternative; rather, he responds to the native speaker cousin with an acknowledgment of her complaint that she is tired and thirsty (both reasons the native speaker has given for admitting her to the house). He then follows up with supportive empathetic expressions ("It's a problem").

Although the non-native speaker guest has been responding to the native speaker cousin's reactions to his reasons for rejecting her request throughout the interaction, Episode 4 provides the first instance in which the non-native speaker addresses the native speaker's expressions of discomfort.

(23) Episode 4

REQUEST 4	NS:	|come on come on just let me in let me in let me sit down and =
	NNS:	[ahhh
	NS:	=take it easy and
Reason for Request		rest for a while I'm thirsty
	NNS:	[ahm
Acknowledgment		yeah
Confirmation	NS:	yeah
Expression of Empathy	NNS:	it's a problem

Confirmation	NS:	yeah it's a problem
Expression of	NNS:	uh it's a problem
Empathy		

Finally, in Episode 5, the non-native speaker responds to the native speaker cousin's last recycling of the request to enter by recycling two of his own reasons: Reasons (b) and (e) (ignorance and powerlessness) — the two reasons which he presumably has evidence to believe are the least likely to offend. At this point the native speaker reluctantly accepts the refusal and leaves.

(24) Episode 5

REQUEST 5	NS:	| let me in an n let me sit uh come in and sit down and wait
Reasons e and b for **Refusal**	NNS:	but I can't decide uh you come in (.) I I can't do that uh I can't what I do this situation (I can't do)
(Reaction) Acceptance of Refusal Complaint/ Farewell	NS:	((sighs)) ah huh huh I don't believe it ok all right ok all right when ya when ya tell when you see Quentin tell him he's a son of a gun ok
		((NS leaves))

5. Interpretation

If we consider the text as a whole and treat this sequence of semantic formulas and their content as the result of a set of non-native speaker steps/heuristics, they could be interpreted as follows:

1. Establish your refusal immediately and clearly (Use of "no", two reasons in first refusal turn)
2. Establish your refusal using a self-effacing approach, stressing your lack of power and resources, and your willingness to help,

if possible (e.g., expression of ignorance, "helpful" alternatives in Episode 1)

3. If 1 and 2 do not prove effective, clarify by clearly asserting what your responsibilities are (End of Episode 1)
4. When your position is clear, return to a polite, self-effacing approach (e.g., powerlessness [Reason e], helpfulness [Alternative 2], as in Episodes 2 and 3)
5. In the face of persistence by the requester,
   a. Notice which approaches result in the most native speaker distress (e.g., "helpful" alternatives in Episodes 1 and 2) and drop them
   b. Address native speaker's concerns empathetically (Episode 4)
   c. Reuse those approaches that have caused the least distress (Reasons b and e, Episode 5)

This sequence of steps represents the work of one learner and is thus of limited generalizability. However, this learner generally conforms to previous characterizations of Japanese learners speaking English in his approach (e.g., use of initial clear on-record speech acts [see Tanaka 1988]) and choice of semantic formulas (e.g., greater reliance on alternatives and empathy in refusals [see Beebe, Takahashi, and Uliss-Weltz 1990]). Thus, it seems worth noting how he employs these resources across interactions in the face of a conversational partner who is reluctant to accept his attempts to refuse gracefully. The result is a sequence of responses which can be characterized individually as generally typical of a (lower or equal status) Japanese, but which, when taken together, reveal a skillful use of these sometimes inappropriate resources in stressful circumstances to achieve a desired outcome.

6. Conclusion

In conclusion, if the interaction is seen as a series of episodes in which the non-native speaker is at some level experimenting with different responses and adjusting his approach as he learns from the native speaker's reactions, the learner reveals a sophisticated procedure for problem solving, in which he tries out a number of different semantic formulas and different content.[22] Thus, we have evidence of a learner who is not simply transferring semantic formulas from the first language, but who is actively searching for successful linguistic and attitudinal resources, and in doing so reveals a wide range of such resources applied in a reasonable problem-solving approach.

Chapter 4
Non-native management of back channels in English refusals

1. Introduction

In this chapter and the next, we move away from a focus on the semantic formulas used by non-native speakers in refusals, approaching the issue of refusals in a cross-cultural setting through the window of minimal verbal and nonverbal information. The decision to include nonverbal aspects of non-native speaker behavior in our investigation stems from a conviction that it is often difficult to interpret the meaning of a reported communicative act when information on nonverbal aspects of the communicative event is not provided.

It is by now well established (e.g., Erickson and Shultz 1982; Goodwin and Goodwin 1987; Kendon 1985, 1994, 1995; Riley 1989; Sheflen 1972, 1973) that much of communicative behavior is nonverbal and that the verbal message of an encounter reflects only one aspect of social competence. Erickson and Shultz (1982) contend that theories of communicative competence that concentrate primarily on records of speech are limited by *inter alia* "underestimating nonverbal and paralinguistic behavior at the expense of the verbal" (p. 215). Similarly, Riley (1989) has observed that "a description of language use is only one dimension of a description of social competence, that not all communicative behavior is verbal and that there are times when actions speak louder than words" (p. 238). Despite such claims, it is still the case that many researchers in second language studies undervalue or ignore the significance of the nonverbal component of an interaction.

Our concern in this chapter is with the act of listening. This is a particularly important locus of investigation for the study of cross-cultural communication in that there is a considerable body of research indicating that meaning is conveyed through minimal vocalizations and nonverbal actions, and that these devices may serve different purposes from culture to culture and situation to situation. As such, it is an area in which misinterpretation of an intended message is likely (cf. Erickson and Shultz's 1982 work on nods, interactional rhythm; ; Fiksdal's 1990 work on timing; Gumperz's 1982 observations on back channels).

In this chapter we will focus on the efforts of non-native speakers to function as effective conversational partners with native speakers, and thus as effective listeners. With this in mind, we will be investigating the use of minimal verbal and nonverbal messages and their role in creating meaning. Our particular emphasis will be on responsive vocalizations and head nods. These features are integral parts of conversation in many cultures despite the fact that, as noted above, they may not be used in precisely the same way.

Hayashi and Hayashi (1991) provide a useful model, similar to that proposed by Yngve (1970),[23] for characterizing listener behavior. Using a cognitive model of interaction, they contrast two conversational channels: 1) the *main channel*, which is the channel used by the speaker, or the person holding the floor; and 2) the *back channel*, which is the channel through which the listener provides information to the speaker, such as attentiveness, agreement, and disagreement. This listener channel is the locus of the behavior with which we are concerned.

It is generally agreed that the cues used in the back channel are important for the establishment and maintenance of a harmonious interaction, for they can signal those aspects of a conversation that lead to harmony (e.g., agreement, understanding, attention). Discussions of back channel behaviors often deal only with simple linguistic cues; however, as Rosenfeld (1987) notes, listener responses often consist of distinctive configurations of nonverbal actions, such as joint nods and vocalizations or multiple versus single head nods. In this chapter, we will be looking at both verbal and nonverbal listener behaviors.

2. Back channels

Back channels are characterized differently by different researchers, who vary in both their formal and functional characterizations of the phenomenon. In this section, we briefly outline some of the more recent approaches.

In an early account, designed to capture both illocutionary and interactional aspects of spoken discourse, Edmondson (1981:148-152) enumerates a number of "discourse-internal illocutions." These include, among other acts, the types of listener behavior that earlier researchers had tagged as back channels. Thus, in addition to acts of greeting, leave-taking, and interrupting, Edmondson identifies the following classes of listener behaviors:

1. Go-Ons — signify that the hearer is attending and is in favor of the speaker continuing
2. Accepts — communicate that an act is heard and understood and is not unacceptable (e.g., *yes, mm*)
3. Exclaims — communicate an emotional reaction to something in the previous discourse or immediate situation, such as doubt, surprise, interest, sympathy
4. Okays — indicate that the listener "is satisfied with a current outcome of an ongoing encounter" (p. 152).

A slightly broader set of listener utterance functions is proposed by Maynard (1989). In her discussion of the interactional management of Japanese conversation, Maynard focuses primarily on listener behavior that occurs "during the turn-internal state" (p.161), that is, without the current speaker relinquishing the turn. In addition to the more commonly analyzed listener vocalizations, she includes both head movement and laughter in her analysis. Working primarily with Japanese conversational data, she identifies six main functions of back channels (pp. 171-172).

1. Continuer — indicates simply that the listener is bypassing the chance to initiate a repair (similar to Edmondson's *Go-Ons*)
2. Display of Content Understanding — is used when there may be doubt on the part of the speaker as to the listener's understanding (similar to Edmondson's *Accepts*)
3. Support Towards the Speaker's Judgment — occurs as a response to a speaker's evaluative statement

4. Agreement — serves as a response to a question or question-like statement; a back channel agreement is not an opportunity to take the floor, only to express agreement
5. Strong Emotional Response — consists of a laugh or exclamation (e.g., *oh no*) indicating more than simple understanding or support (similar to Edmondson's *Exclaims*)
6. Minor Addition, Correction or Request for Information — includes listener comments that change "the quality of the currently activated information" (p. 172), as in listener co-creation of an utterance.

Maynard's classification extends the functions of back channels to include those with more tangible illocutionary force such as agreement, as well as minor additions, corrections, or requests for information — functions which she notes may overlap. This extension of functions to include acts such as repairs results in a broader definition of back channels, similar to that of Duncan and Niederehe (1974) and Yngve (1970). In addition to considering the function of listener responses, Maynard also looks at their distribution, noting that they generally occur in the vicinity of a speaker's pause. Interesting is the fact that back channels are often located near the final syllable of a speaker's utterance when the speaker marks this with a head nod (see section 3 below). Thus, it is possible that both participants may acknowledge one another with nonverbal rather than verbal indications.

Like Maynard, Hayashi and Hayashi (1991) are concerned with those listener behaviors that do not result in the listener taking the floor. They too define a set of categories that include not only acknowledgments of attention and expressions of sympathy, but repair initiations such as requests for clarification and denials.

1. Continuers – do not require a response from the current floor-holder. They consist of the following two subcategories.
    a.   Prompters – nonjudgmental continuers associated with illocutionary acts such as acknowledge, admit, repeat

    b.   Reinforcers – judgmental continuers associated with il-
        locutionary acts such as assert, sympathize, advise,
        blame
2. Repairers – require a response from the current floor-holder.
  They consist of the following two subcategories:
    a.   Clarifiers – nonjudgmental repairers associated with il-
        locutionary acts such as inquire, request
    b.   Claimers – judgmental repairers associated with illocu-
        tionary acts such as deny, disagree

Hayashi and Hayashi treat all back channels as turns, possessing both illocutionary and perlocutionary force, which serve to support the floor.

While Edmondson focuses on spoken English discourse, Maynard's and Hayashi and Hayashi's work is based on interactions in Japanese, with Maynard also contrasting back channel use in English and Japanese. Recently, Clancy, Thompson, Suzuki, and Tao (1996) have investigated the use of what they refer to as reactive tokens in conversations in three languages – English, Japanese, and Chinese. They define a reactive token as "a short utterance that is produced by an interlocutor who is playing a listener's role during the other interlocutor's speakership" (p. 356). Clancy, Thompson, Suzuki, and Tao divide reactive tokens into the following classes (pp. 359-364):

1. Back Channel — "a non-lexical vocalic form" which serves as "a 'continuer' (Schegloff 1982), display of interest, or claim of understanding..."
2. Reactive Expression — "a short non floor–taking lexical phrase or word" uttered by the non-primary speaker; includes forms such as *oh really* or *okay*, as well as assessments such as *exactly*.
3. Collaborative Finish — the completion of a previous speaker's utterance by the non-primary speaker
4. Repetition — the repeating of a portion of the primary speaker's speech

5. Resumptive Opener — a non-lexical element used at turn-initial points to "acknowledge the prior turn and commence a new turn."

Clancy, Thompson, Suzuki, and Tao's definitions rely primarily on the form of the token and its relationship to the surrounding turns. Taken as a whole, Clancy et al.'s reactive tokens overlap to a great extent with Maynard's (and possibly Hayashi and Hayashi's) categories. However, unlike Maynard, they do not include head movements and laughter in their analysis. Also, they restrict the term back channel to continuers, in contrast to much other research, which uses the term to encompass a greater variety of forms and functions.

Thus, there is a range of behaviors which may be considered in listener response back channels. In the following discussion, we will consider both nonverbal (head movements) and verbal listener responses; however, we will restrict the form of verbal tokens to minimal vocalizations (such as *mm, uh huh,* and *yeah*) and brief reactive expressions. On the other hand, we will include a number of functions, as listed below and explained in greater detail in section 3 below:

1. Agreement, including confirmation and a positive response to a yes-no question
2. Acceptance of the speaker's prior utterance
3. Common Back Channel Functions such as continuer, expression of understanding, and expression of support.

These choices are motivated primarily by the fact that the non-native speakers in our study relied a great deal on minimal vocalizations and head movements to convey a wide range of functions.

3. Head movement

In this section we will consider the role of head movement, as one type of back channel, in the communication of listener meaning. After a brief discussion of nods and head shakes, we will present an overview of the illocutionary and interactional functions which we will be considering, supported by examples with both verbal and nonverbal back channels.

Head movements have been mentioned in the literature on English back channels as early as Duncan's work (1973). Recently, in her detailed analysis of characteristics of Japanese conversation, Maynard (1989) devotes an entire chapter to a discussion of head movement as a nonverbal sign. She defines head movements, which include nods and head shakes, in terms of the conversational environments in which they occur and the functions they perform. In Maynard's scheme, listener nods can have several interactional functions, primarily back channel and turn-transition period filler; [24] on the other hand, she sees head shakes (HS) as primarily conveying negation. Maynard notes that back channel head movements may be accompanied by back channel vocalizations.

Maynard deals with head nods separately from verbal back channels. However, the discussion in this section will be concerned with how listener nods (and head shakes) work to perform back channel functions both separately and together with minimal verbalizations in non-native speakers' interactions. The listener nods and head shakes in our data occur in the following environments:

1. separately, with no vocalization
2. with minimal vocalizations, such as *mm, uh huh*
3. with lexical items expressing agreement such as *yes, yeah, ok* (or disagreement, such as *no*)
4. with brief statements such as *it's a problem*

We associate listener nods with illocutionary and interactional functions corresponding to a number of Maynard's back channels and Edmondson's discourse-internal acts. Note for instance that the nods associated with agreement and acceptance in Examples (25) and (27) accompany a verbal affirmative such as *yes* or *ok*. The nods can be seen in Figure 4 (Pictures a-d), where the non-native speaker nod accompanies an accepting *yeah*.

In the remainder of this section, we list the functions of the minimal vocalizations and head movements found in our data, along with examples.

1. Agreement — includes a) brief confirmations (a positive response to a request for confirmation by the speaker) and b) positive responses to yes-no information questions (similar to Maynard's back channel Agreements). Examples from our data are given in (25) and (26). NOD signifies a single nod and NODS signifies multiple nods.

(25) Confirmation

NNS: oh no ((laughing)) wait outside of the house
NS: eh? wait outside?
→ NNS: yeh
→   NOD

(26) Positive response to a yes-no question (see Figure 4)

NS: =do you ever wake up in the morning looking a little pale?
→ NNS: (uhn) yeah yeah
→   NODS ----------
NS: ok
       NODS

2. Acceptance — is a positive response to a speech act requiring an acceptance or a refusal response, such as an invitation or request. Note that Acceptances are not considered back channels by Maynard (1989), Edmondson (1981), or Clancy, Thompson, Suzuki, and Tao (1996). They constitute a substantive contribution and in many (but not all) situations are associated with the listener taking on the role of speaker, as in Example (27) below. However, they can be accomplished nonverbally with just a nod or a nod with minimal vocalization and no further speech.

(27) Acceptance
      NS: I tell you what, we'll just go for a few
                      minutes how's that, do you want to go
                      for just a few minutes?=
→ NNS: =yes.=
→   NOD
      NS: =ok?=
      NNS: =but you don't take you won't take that
                      drug?
      NS: ((sighs)) =ok I won't
      NNS: NODS---

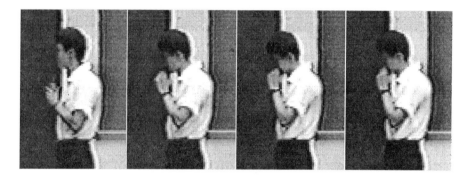

Picture a   Picture b   Picture c   Picture d

Figure 4. Nod

3. Common Back Channel Functions — consist of minimal responses (nod or nod with verbalization such as *mm, yeah, uh
huh*) performed as a) a continuer (or transition filler), b) a
minimal signal of understanding or c) an indication of support,
as in Examples (28), (29), and (30).

(28) Continuer (see Maynard's continuer)

The multiple head nods by the NNS are taken by
the NS as an indication to continue.

	NNS:	um I will call up and tell him about you
		HS
	NS:	uh huh
		NOD
→	NNS:	NODS
	NS:	ok ok um well in the meantime can I wait for him? do you mind if I come in and wait for him and you can call him?

(29) Understanding (see Maynard's display of content understanding)

In this example, nods co-occur with minimal back channels at constituent boundaries; they are taken to indicate attention and, to the extent that no repair is attempted, understanding.

	NS:	ah well do you mind if- I'm I'm his
		NODS
		cousin
→	NNS:	NOD
	NS:	and I'm just passing through Lansing tonight
→	NNS:	mm
→		NODS
	NS:	and I'm I'm on my way to Detroit I'm on a on a business trip
→	NNS:	mm
→		NODS
	NS:	and and uh I'd like to see him I've got about half an hour or so would you mind if I come in and wait for a minute or so an a til he comes back.
	NNS:	ah no wait wait I'm a guest to uh this home I can't uh I don't uh uh um I can't I don't know what uh I do this situation then eh

(30) Support (see Maynard's support toward the speaker's judgment)

In this example, the non-native speaker guest is persuading the native speaker to accompany her to a neighbor's house where the host is, rather than allowing the native speaker to enter the house.

NNS: so please go to him with me
NS: ok all right so come on
         [
→ NNS: NODS------------------uh hhuh
        ((laughing))

NS: all right ok ok all right
        [
→ NNS: NODS----------------- thank you

The non-native speaker's nods and laughter in Example (30) conspire to create a supportive, nonthreatening atmosphere. Note that we have extended the notion of support to include support not only for the native speaker's judgment, but for her feelings as well.

4. Japanese and English nonverbal indicators

Given the focus of our data-base, we now turn to studies comparing back channel behavior by Japanese and English speakers. We first note that the word for back channel in Japanese is *aizuchi*, a non-technical term meaning 'mutual hammering.' S. White (1989) notes that the term "suggests effort to create something valuable" (p. 75). White finds from her data that Japanese use more back channel cues than do American English speakers and that they persist in this be-havior even in cross-cultural interactions. In the cross-cultural con-versations that she examined, she found that the Japanese did not converge to the English pattern (i.e., they maintained the frequency of back channel cues as in their native speech), whereas native speakers of (American) English did converge toward the Japanese norm when speaking in English. Paradoxically, Japanese failure to converge toward American back channel norms may perhaps be explained by reference to the Japanese concept of *omoiyari*, which in White's explanation is the "creation and maintenance of smooth and pleasant human interactions" (p. 67). In order to create this harmonious interaction, one must be sensitive to the views and feelings of one's interlocutor. One way to accomplish this harmonious feeling is through frequent use of vocalizations which indicate attentiveness, understanding and agreement, but which are without meaning in the more traditional sense. An alternative explanation for the greater convergence by Americans to the Japanese norm rather than vice versa is that it is easier to notice the presence of some feature (obvious and frequent head nods) than it is to notice its absence (i.e., less frequent occurrences or non-occurrences).[25]

A second study, dealing with Japanese and American conversations is one by Hayashi (1990). Here differences were found between the two groups in the domain of types of back channel cues. Japanese tended to display many hand and head movements, as well as body movements such as leaning. Americans, on the other hand, used other kinds of feedback devices such as questioning and commenting, which appeared to serve a similar function to back channels. In terms of specific cues, Japanese used primarily vocalizations such as *uhh, soo soo, ahh*, while American English speakers were more likely to make specific verbal comments such as *That's tough, exactly, yeah,* or *I've read that.* Even though these latter may not fit the formal definition of back channel used by many researchers, we maintain that they are functionally equivalent in that their primary goal is to show agreement and to keep the conversation going.[26]

Thus, we have reports on the high frequency of Japanese back channels in conversations in English with native speakers of English and we have descriptions of the Japanese use of minimal vocalizations and nonverbal behavior in the performance of back channels in conversations in Japanese. These reports would lead one to expect that minimal back channel vocalizations and nonverbal signals would play an important role in Japanese conversations in English with native speakers of English.

5. Issues of methodology

In Chapter Two we argued for the need to include videotaped data in research of the type dealt with in this book. This is clearly necessary for an understanding of nonverbal back channels, the aspect of concern in this chapter, as well as for an understanding of nonverbal data in general, the concern of Chapter Five. We maintain that audiotaped data provide only one part of the picture of human interaction and their exclusive use results in an incomplete understanding of the speech act of refusal.

As mentioned in Chapter Two, there are many reasons for the inclusion of videotaped data in speech act research. There are at least two that are important to the discussion in this chapter and the discussion in Chapter Five: 1) people send real messages through nonverbal information (as is shown in this chapter) and 2) nonverbal information aids not only in the negotiation of meaning, but in the management of interlocutor attitude or impression. This latter is the topic of Chapter Five. We argue that nonverbal information (and access to it through videotape) takes on particular importance during face-threatening acts.

6. Analysis

Non-native speaker back channel vocalizations and nods in response to native speaker speech occurred in all of our transcripts. Given the culture-specific nature of many aspects of listener behavior, we asked the following questions:

1. How effectively do these Japanese non-native speakers of English coordinate their back channel vocalizations and nods with native speaker speech?

2. How are non-native speaker back channels distributed across their refusal negotiations?

3. What kinds of problems, if any, do these non-native speakers experience in producing appropriate back channels in English?

6.1. *Ability*

The data that we have examined from Japanese learners of English showed these learners to have considerable ability as English listeners, coordinating minimal vocalizations and nods with the ongoing flow of native speaker speech. Coordination of back channel responses in a second language is not as easy as it may seem. Hinds (1978, cited in LoCastro 1987) observed that non-native speakers of Japanese may overuse back channels or use them in the wrong place when speaking Japanese, causing the native speaker of Japanese to stop talking.

In our data, we noted that a lower proficiency Japanese speaker of English encountered problems coordinating head movement and gesture with verbal message, as Example (31) indicates.

(31) Lack of coordination of non-verbal and verbal messages

```
        1      NS:    you will go skydiving NODS
→       2      NNS:   NOD HS ah no
                             HS--
        3      NS:    no?
        4      NNS:   NODS
        5      NS:    no no what ((laughs)) no you don't like to
                      skydive?
→       6      NNS:   NODS skydiving HS no
                            HS-------
        7      NS:    skydiving no ((laughs))
                                  [
        8      NNS:              NODS
        9      NS:    oh are y- do you not like to skydive?
                                 HS------------------
                      you do not like to skydive?
                      HS-----------------------
→      10      NNS:   no
→                     NODS
```

In line 2, in response to the native speaker's indication that the non-native speaker will go skydiving, the non-native speaker first nods, then shakes his head. In line 6, he nods, repeats the native speaker's last word, "skydiving," and then shakes his head (see Pictures a-f, Figure 5).

Clearly, the non-native speaker wishes to indicate a disinclination to skydive; however, his use of a nod before a head shake results in a pair of confusing, if not contradictory messages. In line 10, he coordinates his negative response with a nod.[27] It is likely that the nod accompanying a negative word is a result of transfer from Japanese, where a *yes* or *no* response to a question indicates agreement or disagreement with the proposition rather than correspondence with the valence of the proposition, as in English. Thus, a Japanese will usually respond to a question such as "Are you not going?" with "Yes, I'm not going" (as will speakers of many other languages), whereas a native speaker of English will respond with "No, I'm not going." In Example (31), it appears that the non-native speaker was able to utter an appropriate negative, *no*, but was unable to coordinate this with the appropriate head movement. The subtle movements are difficult to see in still shots. However, to obtain an idea of his head shake, follow the sequence from a to f (Figure 5). In picture (a), there is little of the non-native speaker's right side of the face visible, in pictures (b), (c), and (d) more of his face becomes visible until in pictures (e) and (f), there is less. In the latter two, the head has moved to a position comparable to the position in picture (a).

On the other hand, the more advanced non-native speakers were consistently quite proficient in their coordination of nods and head shakes with meaning. For example, they used nods for acknowledgments or apologies and head shakes for disagreements or refusals, timing them properly, even when the two appeared together, as in the "yes-but" disagreements preferred by many native speakers of English (Gumperz, Jupp, and Roberts 1979), illustrated in Example (32).

(32) Yes-but disagreement

    1   NS: and I was win in Chi- Chicago the night before
                    I'm beat let me in let me sit down and wait

                   for Quentin this is ridiculous
                        [[
2   NNS: ahh   so
                                  SMALL NOD
                   feel very sorry yeah but I so I cannot
                        NODS   HS
                   decide this door open

Picture a   Picture b   Picture c   Picture d   Picture e   Picture f

Figure 5. Head shakes

In Example (32), the non-native speaker's speech illustrates the proficiency with which a more advanced non-native speaker coordinates
nods and head shakes with communicative intent, in this case a refusal. He provides an empathetic nod with an apology (*sorry*) followed by a head shake with *but*, which introduces an excuse expressing a refusal.

   Further, these advanced non-native speakers placed back channel
vocalizations at speaker clause boundaries or other transition-relevant
points, often in the absence of speaker pauses to mark those boundaries, as was seen in Example (28).[28]

6.2. Distribution: High frequency contexts

Back channels occurred both during the more cordial segments of conversation and during many of the less harmonious periods as in Example (33).[29]

(33) Back channels

The native speaker is attempting to persuade the non-native speaker to let her (the native speaker) into the house.

	1	NS:	=let me sit down and take it easy and
	2	NNS:	ahm
			[
	3	NS:	rest for a while I'm thirsty
→	. 4	NNS:	yeah
	5	NS:	yeah
	6 *	NNS:	it's a problem
			NODS
	7	NS:	yeah it's a problem
			NODS----------
	8 *	NNS:	uh it's a problem
			NODS-------------
	9	NS:	I'm tired I'm beat
→	10	NNS:	uhm yeah
→			NOD

In this example the non-native speaker intersperses *yeahs* and nods (lines 4 and 10) with explicit expressions of empathy (lines 6 and 8), accompanied by nods.[30] However, the non-native speaker's intent is clearly one of refusal. (Expressions of empathy are indicated by asterisks.)

This use of back channels seems to support the claims by researchers such as Hayashi (1990), LoCastro (1987), and S. White (1989) that Japanese use back channels primarily as an empathic or supportive response. This contrasts with Americans, who use minimal vocalizations frequently as a continuer (Schegloff 1982).[31]

6.3. *Distribution: A low frequency context*

Despite the occurrence of back channels across both cordial and less harmonious stretches of discourse, neither the frequency nor the nature of back channels necessarily remains constant across an interaction. In fact, the number of back channels (and back channel nods) produced in our data dropped dramatically in some initial refusal situations. Example (34) occurs during the non-native speaker's first refusal (See Chapter Three). It is accompanied by an increase in the non-native speaker's speaking volume.

(34) First refusal

1	NNS:	((slightly louder)) uh-uh if uh you want to meet uh
2	NS:	I can't believe this
		[
3	NNS:	him
4	NS:	I can't believe this this is my cousin this is my cousin
		[
5	NNS:	but I don't know you
		[
6	NS:	we grew up together we went fishing together
7	NNS:	uh HS
8	NS:	you mean to tell me I can't even come=
9	NS:	= in his house
10	NNS:	HS (but) I don't know you are cousin I don't know HS
11	NS:	well who uh a- a- a- a- a- uh-uh- that's not my problem
12	NNS:	oh yeah

```
13  NS:      that's not my problem you don't know?  what
             do you what are you talking about=
             [
14  NNS:      nn
15  NS:      = this is Quentin's my cousin what are you
             doing
16  NNS:     oohnn
             HS (slight)
17  NS:      you're not going to let me in his house=
                              [
18  NNS:                         uhh
19  NS:      =I can't believe this
             [        [
20  NNS:      I       said
             it's my business I now I homestay
             yeh I cannot door open
             NODS
             [
21  NS:      what do you mean it's your business who are
             you how do I know you're not a burglar
22  NNS:     ((softly)) no (?)
                      HS
       ((END of the NNS'S RAISED VOLUME))
```

This segment is filled with non-native speaker vocalizations and head shakes, for example, lines 7 (*uh* HS), 16 (*oohnn* HS), and the appropriate *no* with HS in line 22. However, there are virtually no back channel nods nor typical continuers or displays of content understanding or support (*mms, uh huhs*, nods). There is one back channel-style utterance (*oh yeah* in line 12), which is associated with agreement. However, in this instance the use of *oh yeah* (with falling intonation) as a back channel is inappropriate. In fact, with rising intonation, it could be taken as a challenge.

On the other hand, once the non-acceptance was established (as indicated by the fact that the native speaker finds it necessary to re-cycle the request; see line 2 in Example 35), the non-native speaker resumed back channels, even when called upon to repeat the refusal.

The following example picks up at the end of the previous example, as the non-native speaker lowers his voice.

(35) Back channels

```
        1    NNS:    ((softly)) no ( )
                              HS
   ((END of the NNS'S RAISED VOLUME))
        2    NS:     I'm a oh boy boy Quentin's not going to
                     hear the last of this │come on let me in
        3    NNS:    aoo
        4    NS:     come on I've been traveling all the way
                     from Muskegon
→       5    NNS:    oh yeah
→                    NODS
                       [
        6    NS:         and I was win in Chi- Chicago the night
                     before I'm beat let me in let me sit down
                     and wait for Quentin this is ridiculous
                                      [           [
        7    NNS:               ahh        so
                               SMALL NOD
                     I feel very sorry yeah but I so I cannot
                                   NODS      HS
                     decide this door open
        8    NS:     oh come on
                     NODS
→       9    NNS:    yeah NODS
       10    NS:     just let me in
                     NODS-------
→      11    NNS:    yeah uh NODS
→                    NOD
       12    NS:     just yeah let me in
                     NODS--------------
       13    NNS:    yeah oh so I think you had better to go
                     NOD
                     neighbor's house to uh to meet him
```

We suggest two possible explanations for the decrease in back channels and nods during initial refusals, both of which may lead to different types of misunderstanding. One possibility is that linguistic back channels and nods indicating support or empathy may weaken the refusal. In the cousin situation, the native speaker was particularly aggressive and the non-native speaker began with a strong refusal without any socially ameliorating signals that could indicate ambivalence.

A second possible explanation for the decrease in back channels and nods during an initial refusal is the danger of the refusal not being understood and thus being taken as something other than a refusal. As discussed below, back channels such as *yeah* can be ambiguous. In our situations, the combination of the stress of refusing, the speed of the native speaker's English — which was rife with direct and indirect offers and requests, and the desire to be clear made it particularly risky to show support and empathy during the initial refusal. In negotiating a negative face-threatening speech act, the Japanese non-native speakers in our study may have opted initially for clarity, followed by a resumption of back channels after they felt they had made their point and the threat of misinterpretation had passed.

Thus, these more advanced Japanese used back channels conveying understanding during native speaker explanations and empathy during native speaker stress. Back channels were generally withheld during speech acts in which an indication of a positive response could be taken as an acceptance, with all the commitments entailed thereby. In addition to negotiating their way through a relatively tricky speech act with a sometimes aggressive native speaker, these non-native speakers often situated back channels at points at which they might be expected to show support and empathy for the native speaker and to mitigate the negative effect of the native speaker's loss of face.

6.4. *Problems*

We have discussed some of the uses of back channel vocalizations and nods by non-native speakers of English. However, these back channels were not always used so effectively by this group. Problems in the use and interpretation of linguistic back channels by proficient non-native speakers of English have been reported by Gumperz (1990), Hatch (1992), and Luthy (1983). The occasions of misuse reveal areas in which even more advanced non-native speakers of English may encounter problems. These include the use of *yeah* as a back channel and the use of back channel vocalizations and nods during native speaker eliciting acts such as invitations.

6.4.1. *Yeah* as a back channel

As should be evident from a consideration of Maynard's (1989) and Edmondson's (1981) lists of back channel functions, a back channel token may sometimes serve more than one function within a speech community, and the same token may have different ranges of interpretation from community to community.

Yeah, yes, and even *uh huh* are some of the back channels used regularly by native speakers of English. Unlike *mm, hmm, umm,* etc., *yeah, yes,* and *uh huh* are often used by native speakers of British and American English to signal agreement. This is not necessarily the case for speakers of other varieties of English or for non-native speakers of English speaking English. For instance, Gumperz (1990) has shown that for speakers of Indian English, back channel *yes* and *no* are used mostly as a way of showing attention to the speaker's previous positive or negative statement. This difference in use can result in serious miscommunication.[32]

LoCastro (1987) cites a similar misunderstanding involving a native speaker of Japanese. As reported in *The Japan Times*, a Mr. Ishida was accused of agreeing with FBI undercover agents when they told him that there was no choice but to steal the information he was seeking. The defense counsel claimed that Ishida used *yeah* and *uh huh* not to signal agreement, but rather to show that he was attending to what was being said.

It may be that many Japanese non-native speakers of English are aware of the dangers of using *yeah, yes,* or *uh huh* as a back channel.[33] S. White (1989) mentions that the Japanese non-native speakers of English in her study produced the same back channel tokens as native speakers except for *yeah*, which did not occur. Likewise, in most of our transcripts, back channels are expressed exclusively by minimal verbalizations such as *mm, mm hm, uh huh*. However, in one of our transcripts, the non-native speaker made relatively effective use of *yeah* to fulfill primary vocalization functions conveying understanding and empathy (see sections 6.2 and 6.3 for examples).

On the other hand, the difficulty in controlling the possible messages sent by back channel *yeah* is highlighted when the same non-native speaker responds to a native speaker's sarcastic thanks with *yeah* and a nod, as in Example (36).

(36) Back channel *yeah*

> The non-native speaker has suggested that the native speaker go to the neighbors' house where Mr. Quentin is visiting at the moment. However, when the native speaker asks for directions, the non-native speaker admits that he doesn't know where the house is.

1	NS:	so what am I supposed to do drive around?
		I don't know his neighbors either
2	NNS:	uh y- you can uh go by walk
3	NS:	thank you thank you very much very=
		[[[
4	NNS:	yeah yeah yeah
		NODS NODS NODS
5	NS	= kind of you

The three *yeahs* (line 4) after the native speaker's sarcastic thanks (line 3) stand out as unusual. And they call attention to two problems. First, the non-native speaker does not seem to perceive the native speaker's intended sarcasm. If he does, he is unable to provide an appropriate response (in this situation, perhaps an apology or an apologetic vocalization). In either case, the non-native speaker reveals an inability to deal appropriately with a sarcastic interaction in English. Second, the non-native speaker uses the English back channel *yeah* inappropriately in a situation in which it could be misconstrued.[34] This *yeah* with its nod could be interpreted by a native speaker as a sarcastic and inflammatory response.

Notice that if the non-native speaker had stuck with neutral *mms*, without nods, this response might have been less noticeable, and the non-native speaker's problems with the native speaker's sarcasm might have been missed. General Japanese reliance on simple vocalizations and nods when speaking English may allow many problems in inferencing to pass undetected.

6.4.2. Primary vocalizations

However, problems can arise even with simple primary vocalizations (especially those accompanied by nods) if they occur during the performance of a speech act (e.g., an invitation or request). This is particularly so when there is an expectation of an acceptance or refusal, with reference to which hearer responses will be interpreted.

That even primary vocalizations can send the wrong message in such situations, especially when accompanied by nods, is shown in Example (37).

(37) Primary vocalizations and nods

> The non-native speaker has already refused the native speaker's invitation to a party with drugs that evening, claiming that her friend is having a birthday party, to which both the non-native speaker and native speaker are invited and which she wishes to attend.

	1	NS:	no no ok all right ((breath)) weell, uhh I'd better go to this party cause I promised my friends, I promised my friends, if you like I can drop you off at your friend at the at your friend's house
→	2	NNS:	mmhm
→			NODS-
	3	NS:	would you mind that? do you wanta do that?
→	4	NNS:	mm
→			NOD

```
       5  NS:    and then I can pick you up later?
                 NODS
→      6  NNS:   mm hm
→                NODS-
       7  NS:    do you wanta do that? ok we'll do that ok so I'll
                 drop you off at your friend's house
→      8  NNS:   NODS
       9  NS:    ok so let's go
      10  NNS:   uh no
                      HS (1/2)
      11  NS:    I- I'm gonna drop you off at your friend's=
                                               [
      12  NNS:                                  nn?
                                                HS-----
      13  NS:    =house
      14  NNS:   uh no no no no no
                 HS-----------------
```

The successive *mms, mm hms,* and nods (lines 2, 4, 6, 8) that occur during the native speaker's offer of a ride to the non-native speaker's friend's house lead the native speaker to believe that her offer has been accepted. However, it is clear from the non-native speaker's reaction in lines 10, 12, and 14 that she did not intend to accept the native speaker's offer. Perhaps she misunderstood the native speaker's intentions. However, whether the non-native speaker understood the native speaker completely or not, she obviously intended her nods and *mm hms* as pleasant, perhaps supportive back channels similar to those of the defendant discussed by LoCastro (1987). The result is an instance of miscommunication.

Thus, even primary vocalizations can send an unintended message when they are uttered at a point where they can be interpreted as a response to a speech act that "invites by convention a response or sequel" (Austin 1975: 117).

7. Conclusion

In this chapter we have considered some uses of back channel vocalizations and nods by Japanese in face threatening situations with native speakers of English. In casual conversations, the proficient non-native speakers in this study use back channel vocalizations and nods extensively and quite successfully to indicate attention, understanding, support, and empathy. However, they run into occasional problems with choice of back channel token and with performance of back channels during speech acts such as offers which set up an expectation of a response intended as acceptance or refusal.

These problems serve to focus attention on several aspects of non-native speaker nonverbal communication. With respect to Japanese non-native speakers in particular, it demonstrates both the effectiveness with which these proficient Japanese non-native speakers of English use back channels and nods in most English interactions and the extent to which a misunderstanding may pass unnoticed because of Japanese reliance on primary vocalizations. More generally, it illustrates the amount of work involved in performing the interactional and social aspects of a delicate speech act such as a refusal and the potential for miscommunication that exists outside the verbal message during negotiation of a speech act.[35]

The extent to which minimal vocalizations and nods may carry critical components of an interactant's message (in situations such as those described above) indicates the importance of identifying nonverbal sources of difficulty for non-native speakers, as well as those areas or situations in which miscommunication is most likely to occur.

Chapter 5
Nonverbal behavior in non-native English refusals

1. Introduction

As shown in Chapter Four, utterances devoid of linguistic content (such as those made up of minimal vocalizations) can contribute to the negotiation of speech acts. Another communicative resource that does not involve language and that may have an impact on speech act negotiation is nonverbal behavior, which can be used not only to transmit meaning, but to affect the tone of an interaction as well.

In Chapter Two we discussed briefly several ways in which access to information on nonverbal behavior can affect our understanding of an interaction. In Chapter Four we considered some functions of head movements, one type of nonverbal behavior frequently used to convey listener meaning. In this chapter we will focus on the role that other types of nonverbal behavior may assume in native/non-native interaction, specifically in a face-threatening situation.

As demonstrated in Chapter Four, nonverbal behavior can accompany an interactant's speech or occur on its own. Instances of responsive nonverbal behavior by a listener during the speech of his/her interlocutor are common, as evidenced by the role of back channel nods. Also, when associated with silence on the part of a floorholder, nonverbal acts can communicate a propositional and/or illocutionary meaning. For instance, when an initiating act is performed, all things being equal, an addressee's silence is usually interpreted as carrying meaning in terms of a response. Thus, when silence occurs after a request, invitation, offer, or suggestion, it may signal an attempt by the addressee to perform a potentially face-threatening refusal politely, "off-record" (Sifianou 1997). Clues as to the source of a silent addressee's difficulty in responding and the nature of the difficult-to-articulate response can be transmitted through nonverbal behavior (e.g., the in-breath and pained expression that often precede or constitute a refusal in Japanese).

In addition to the role that it can perform during a floorholder's silence, nonverbal behavior may also be used to affect the linguistic message when it accompanies speech. Neu (1990) notes that verbal messages can be reinforced or undermined by the nonverbal message. She gives as an example someone slouching in a chair reading a newspaper, saying "I'm listening." Focusing on the intentional use of nonverbal behavior, Edmondson (1981) claims that "nonverbal clues are of great significance in accomplishing and modifying the effect of verbal communication" (p. 78). The need for interactants to modify the effect of verbal communication may be particularly important when face-threatening speech acts are involved since in those instances, inappropriate pragmalinguistic and sociopragmatic behavior may have particularly serious consequences.

Thus, nonverbal behavior can express a message on its own or modify a concurrently produced verbal message. As such, it constitutes a potentially powerful resource for non-native speakers, who are often aware of a need to convey a certain degree of respect, concern, or politeness but lack the necessary linguistic resources to do so.

In this chapter, we will consider some of the relevant claims regarding the kinds of use to which nonverbal behavior may be put, as well as some of the differences in its use across cultures. We will then examine three interactions between Japanese non-native speakers of English and a native speaker of English in which each of the non-native speakers refuses an offer by the native speaker. In these interactions the non-native speakers' verbal messages are essentially the same, but these messages are affected by their nonverbal behavior.

2. Nonverbal behavior

In this section, we will consider some of the attested functions of nonverbal behavior, as well as differences between native speakers of English and native speakers of Japanese in the frequency and function of particular nonverbal behaviors.

2.1. Strategic uses of nonverbal behavior

Many different nonverbal channels can be used to convey meaning (e.g., gaze direction, facial expression, head movement, gesture, posture). A number of approaches to classifying the types of communicative behavior regularly expressed through nonverbal channels have been proposed (notably Ekman and Friesen 1969; Mehrabian 1972; Patterson 1994; see Rozelle, Druckman, and Baxter 1997 for a discussion). Among these, Patterson's (1994) approach is particularly useful, as it includes classes of behavior employed in influencing the impression communicated by an interlocutor. Patterson categorizes nonverbal behaviors according to their communicative functions. He is especially interested in capturing the strategic uses to which nonverbal behavior can be put, where *strategic use* refers to deliberate, managed behaviors which can be used to override negative affective reactions. Rather than focusing on one type of nonverbal behavior, Patterson describes constellations of behaviors associated with particular strategic functions or meanings. His categories of managed behavior patterns include: 1) regulation of interaction, 2) exertion of social control, 3) a presentational function, and 4) affect management. Two of these categories, regulation of interaction and exertion of social control, are relevant to our purposes.

The first of Patterson's types of managed behavior, *regulation of interaction,* deals with the "development, maintenance, and termination of a communicative exchange" (Rozelle, Druckman, and Baxter 1997: 79). It is associated with "specific behavioral adjustments designed to facilitate or inhibit interaction" (Patterson 1994: 280). Regulating behaviors include an increase or decrease in gaze directed at a partner and greater or lesser facial responsiveness. Thus, a decrease in gaze and facial responsiveness (particularly when coupled with other behaviors such as interruption) has been observed to result in less conversational initiation by conversational partners and negative attitudes towards the interaction. Conversely, attentive listener behavior as conveyed by an increase in gaze and facial responsiveness may inspire positive feelings with respect to the interaction.

Patterson defines the second strategic function of nonverbal behavior, *exertion of social control,* as the "managed expression of nonverbal involvement that is designed to influence an interaction partner" (p. 282). This includes showing power and dominance, providing feedback and reinforcement, and creating a specific impression. Particularly pertinent are nonverbal behaviors associated with attempts to persuade. High involvement behaviors such as increases in gaze, nods, gestures, and facial activity have been associated with persuasive behavior and positive impression management.

Thus, co-occurrences of nonverbal behaviors have been associated with the strategic regulation of interaction and with the management of impressions, especially with an eye to persuasion.[36] Note that researchers such as Patterson do not claim that there are fixed constellations of nonverbal behaviors which are immutably associated with particular interpretations, only that such associations have been attested. As such, they provide a backdrop against which to interpret the nonverbal behaviors of interest to us in this chapter.

2.2. Cross-cultural differences in nonverbal behavior

While research on employment of nonverbal behavior in communication and impression management indicates that this is a universal function of nonverbal behavior, it is important to keep in mind that the role of many specific behaviors is culturally determined.[37]

Nonverbal behavior may carry different degrees of importance and serve different functions across cultures. There has been extensive research indicating that, while there are some universals in nonverbal behavior (e.g., certain facial expressions seem to convey the same feeling or attitude in all cultures), the use or distribution and the significance of these behaviors is culturally determined. This can be illustrated by studies comparing facial expressions and regulatory head movements produced by native speakers of English and native speakers of Japanese.

Ekman (1978) has claimed that while some facial expressions convey the same message across cultures, their use may differ considerably. He reports on a study of Japanese and American college students watching a stress-inducing film. Ekman found that when the students watched the film alone, their expressions were virtually the same; however, when an experimenter was present, there was little correspondence between the expressions of the Japanese and

Americans. On the whole, the Japanese were found to mask unpleasant emotions more than Americans.

The use of regulatory head movements has also been shown to differ in Japanese and American conversations. As Maynard (1989) found in her study of Japanese and American nods and head shakes, while head movement is an important nonverbal behavior in conversational regulation in both cultures, it is assigned different values and social meanings in each. In Japan, among other functions, the frequent use of nods by both interactants serves to indicate "constant and consistent rapport building" (p. 212), with speakers frequently using nods to mark clause and turn end markers (see also Kita 1998). While American listeners also use nods (albeit less frequently than Japanese), according to Maynard, they tend to rely on them much less frequently to mark clauses and turn ends, employing them more often for emphasis or dramatic effect.

Thus, there are often differences not only in the types of nonverbal expression manifested in particular situations, but also in the messages that nonverbal resources may be used to convey.

In addition, the relative value placed on nonverbal and verbal expression in different cultures may vary, especially during the negotiation of a face-threatening act. Saville-Troike (1989) has observed that Japanese depend on wordless communication in emotionally loaded situations. Given this Japanese reluctance to express unpleasant information verbally, it would not be surprising to find that, in addition to relying on context and their interlocutor's inferencing ability, Japanese might count on nonverbal resources to somehow mitigate the effect of a face-threatening act. Takahashi and Beebe (1993) state that "it has generally been observed that the Japanese try to express regret, for instance, through nonverbal and/or paralinguistic means such as facial expressions, tone of voice, sighs, hesitance and so forth." They go on to say that Japanese prefer "less verbally explicit expressions, particularly in face-threatening situations," depending instead on the nonverbal message (p.143).

In contrast, it appears that Americans tend to rely on language in responding to face-threatening situations. Takahashi and Beebe (1993) suggest that "American culture promotes explicit verbal means of correcting, refusing, or disagreeing and thus encourages explicit verbal means of undoing the threat to face that the explicit correction, refusal, or disagreement poses" (p. 144). Thus, Americans seem to concentrate on the verbal content of the message in a face-threatening act, while Japanese resort more often to the nonverbal channel to establish a message.

Because of the importance attached to nonverbal messages by Japanese, particularly in socially threatening situations, information on the nonverbal behavior of interactants may be essential to understanding the negotiation of a face threatening act.

Thus, we are left with two considerations in examining the nonverbal behavior of three non-native speakers: 1) that nonverbal behaviors can serve strategic purposes and 2) that, given the reported use of nonverbal behavior by Japanese to mitigate threats to an addressee's face, heavy reliance on nonverbal resources may reflect attempts to manage or mitigate a potential refusal. These considerations, coupled with our observation of the striking difference in impression left by the three non-native speakers in the role play mentioned above, give rise to several questions:

1. What nonverbal behaviors does each of these three non-native speakers exhibit in negotiating the refusal?

2. In what ways do these non-native speakers' nonverbal behaviors differ from each other?

3. What type of message(s) does their nonverbal behavior convey?

In an attempt to gain some insight into the answers to these questions, we will first look at transcripts of each of the three interactions, with nonverbal behavior marked in capitals. We will then compare the nonverbal behaviors of each of the three non-native speakers.

3. The data

The observed contrast between the verbal and nonverbal messages in three role plays of the same situation illustrates the potential importance of nonverbal behavior in non-native speakers' interactions with native speakers. In the role play situations given in the examples in this chapter, the native speaker host mother offers to pierce the visiting non-native speaker's ears. In each of the videotaped interactions, the non-native speakers performed a relatively acceptable linguistic refusal. However, one look at the videotapes shows that each of the three non-native speakers employed quite different nonverbal devices for carrying the act off. In what follows we present the transcripts of the three interactions.[38] In section 4 we present pictures of the gestures of these three individuals. Information on the nonverbal resources that these non-native speakers drew upon while engaged in refusing has been transcribed. This includes instances of non-native speaker head movements, gestures, and posture.

(38)   Rie = Japanese woman; Ann = American woman

1   Ann: yeah, y'd l- wouldja like to get your ears pierced like that?

2   Rie: oh yes
            NOD

3   Ann: you'd like to? good I'll call my girlfriend, my g-
            see see what my girlfriend did to my ears?

4   Rie: NOD

5   Ann: isn't that wonderful? all these studs? I'm gonna call my girlfriend right now. ok?   all right?
            [

6   Rie: wait a minute
            LH UP FROM ELBOW

7   Ann: what, what,

8   Rie: I want to m pierce my ears but mm someday, mm NOD

9   Ann: oh but she can do it right now, she does it really well, she see see what she said I mean it doesn't hurt it just hurts y'know it's a little sting? and then it's all over? and she does it really well,

10 Rie: oh no but uh
                      [

11 Ann: my ears were only infected for three months ((laughs))

12 Rie: oh but I nn I'm not determined yet, nn

| 13 | Ann: | you're not determined yet, |

13 Ann: you're not determined yet,
14 Rie: umm yeh NOD
15 Ann: uum you haven't decided (.) but it but I thought you said you liked those. on the television.
16 Rie: nn
17 Ann: don'tcha wanna look like a rock star ((popping fingers twice))? yeah, I mean all your friends would (.) all your friends would would I mean you would be the only one on your block (.) right? you would be the first person to have your ears done like that, sure you don't want to? I can call my girlfriend (.) right away,
18 Rie: oohh nn no thank you very much
19 Ann: are you sure?
20 Rie: NOD
21 Ann: sure? I c'n we c'n just do it and it just takes twenty minutes, it doesn't take a long time
22 Rie: ohhh no hh
23 Ann: I can call her
24 Rie: no thank you
25 Ann: ok,   ok, all right,
                [
26 Rie: NOD

(39)   Ryo = Japanese man

1 Ann: y' know what?=
              [
2 Ryo: LEANS FORWARD-->
3 Ann: =see- see the way I have my ears pierced
              HAND TO EAR---------------------------
              [
4 Ryo: LEANING FORWARD----------------------
5 Ann: doesn't that look cool?
6 Ryo: LEANS FURTHER, PEERS, HAND TO OWN EAR

7 Ann: see the way I have my ears pierced? remember
        I've got four=
8 Ryo: um
        LEANING FORWARD
9 Ann: =I've got four holes here in this ear?
10 Ryo: yeh
11 Ann: wouldn't you like t' have ears like that?
12 Ryo: ((laughs)) no no
                ARM OUT ---
                PALM DOWN
                WAVES HAND
                LEANS BACK
13 Ann: are y' sure?=
14 Ryo: =HS no
            HS
        ARM OUT
15 Ann: I could call my girlfriend 'n
                        [
16 Ryo: no no stop
                        ARM OUT
        ((laughs))
17 Ann: ((laughs)) really I can I mean you know (.) she
        c'n do it she c'n do it in an in an hour and it'll be
        all over
18 Ryo: uh
        ARM WAVE
19 Ann: wouldn't you like to have your ears pierced?
20 Ryo: no no no
        ARM WAVE
21 Ann: it's so cool
22 Ryo: ah I don't want to be pierced   (.)   my ears
            HAND TO EAR ------------------------
            JERKY MOTION   STOMP
23 Ann: you're sure,
24 Ryo: yeh
        NOD

25   Ann: are you sure?

26   Ryo: uh

27   Ann: I mean have you really thought about it? you're
             sure you don't want to?

28   Ryo: no I don't want
             HAND ACROSS BODY
             WAVES

29   Ann: ok, ok,=

30   Ryo: =ok?=

31   Ann: =all right, ((laughs)) ok,

(40)   Mie = Japanese woman

1   Ann: oh you like the way my ears ears are done? see
            the way they do it on MTV,
            isn't that great?
            [

2   Mie: LEANS FORWARD SLIGHTLY
            MOVES TOWARD NS 2X

3   Mie: n- n- it- it's interesting
            NODS
            POINTS TO "TV"------------
                    [

4   Ann: yeah
            y'know y'know what, I c'n we can get your ears
            pierced exactly like mine y'see that?=
                                    BRUSHES
                                    HAIR BACK
                                    SHOWS EAR--------
            =isn' that nice? y'like that? I c'n call my
            SHOWING EAR----------
            girlfriend right now
            'n she c'n she c'n come over in 20 minutes
            [

5   Mie: HEAD SHAKE--------------------------------
            HAND WAVE--------------------------------
            HEAD TURNS AWAY---------------------

```
6   Mie:   no thank you
           HEAD SHAKE-
           HAND WAVES
           HEAD AWAY---
7   Ann:   are you sure?
8   Mie:   uh yes I- I don't (want) to  pierce my ears=
           NOD HAND WAVE
                           HAND TO EAR-------
           HEAD AWAY-----------
9          =I like just looking ((laughs)) this TV
              POINTS AT "TV"----------------------
10  Ann:   y- you you like you like MTV?
11  Mie:   yes yes but I don't (like) to pierce  my ears
           NOD---
           POINTS    HAND       HAND  HAND
                     WAVE       TO EAR WAVE
                     HEAD
                     AWAY
12  Ann:   y'y' sure?
13  Mie:   NODS
14  Ann:   cuz it cuz it looks so cool doesn't it look cool?
           doesn't it look so nice? isn't this
           great?
              [
15  Mie:   but              but no (.) NOD
           HAND WAVE -------------
           HEAD SHAKE ------------
16  Ann:   you're sure, cuz I c'n call my girlfriend, I mean
           you can have it done right here and now
           REACHES FOR "PHONE"
17  Mie:   eh hh mm  no
                       HAND WAVE
                       HEAD TURN
18  Ann:   you sure?
19  Mie:   NODS
20  Ann:   absolutely?
```

```
21  Mie:    n?
            LEANS SLIGHTLY
            EAR TOWARD NS
            MOVES FORWARD
22  Ann:    are you absolutely sure?  you you've definitely
            decided?  I c'n call my girlfriend
            REACHES FOR "PHONE"
23  Mie:    no ((laugh))
            HAND WAVE---
            HEAD SHAKE
24  Ann:    WITHDRAWS HAND FROM PHONE
25  Mie:    thank you=
            NODS------

            [
26  Ann:    NODS------ =no, you're sure, ok, all right, ok,
```

These transcripts reveal that a wide range of nonverbal behaviors, including nods, head shakes, and head turns and a variety of gestures, and posture shifts (particularly leaning) occur during the non-native speakers' interactions with the native speaker of English.

4. Comparison of non-native speakers' nonverbal behavior

As can also be seen from the transcripts, there is little to distinguish the semantic formulas used by each non-native speaker to carry out the refusal. For example, subjects generally responded with an explicit "no," which was repeated throughout the interaction (Example 38, lines 10, 18; Example 39, lines 12, 14, 16, 20; Example 40, lines 6, 15, 17, 23), with a "no thank you" in two of the three cases (Example 38, line 18; Example 40, line 6). Also, all provided one additional bit of more substantive information such as a put-off ("I want to m pierce my ears but mm someday" [Example 38, line 8]; "oh but I nn I'm not determined yet, nn" [Example 38, line 12]); or a reason "I don't want to be pierced (.) my ears" [Example 39, line 22]; "uh yes I-I don't (want) to pierce my ears I like just looking the TV" [Example 40, line 8]). Apart from some back channels and a few instances of negotiation of meaning, these constitute the linguistic contributions of the three non-native speakers.

On the other hand, although there is little linguistic variation to differentiate the responses, there is considerable variation in the non-verbal arena. Furthermore, the impression that is conveyed as a result of this variation differs considerably from speaker to speaker.

We now turn to the nonlinguistic differences among these three Japanese refusers.

4.1. *Rie's nonverbal behavior*

In Example (38), the non-native speaker, Rie, a woman, relies primarily on language (and an unchanging demeanor) to convey her message and any associated attitudes. With the exception of a few back channel-type nods (lines 2, 4, 14), one gesture (line 6), and a constant smile, she uses few specific nonverbal actions. In fact, during almost the entire interaction, she

   a. remains practically immobile
   b. holds her hands behind her back, and
   c. smiles.

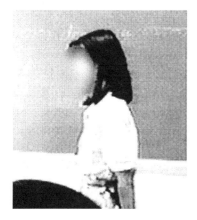 

      Picture a   Picture b

Figure 6. Rie's posture

Even when the native speaker, Ann, uses a phrase that the non-native speaker most likely missed ("you would be the only one on your block, right?" in the middle of line 17), Rie gives no nonverbal signal (e.g., a shift in posture, change in expression) that she might not have understood. The impression is of a pleasant, contained, gracious conversationalist. Examples of Rie's posture and gesture can be seen in Pictures a and b, respectively (Figure 6).

In contrast, the non-native speakers in Examples (39) and (40) use posture (e.g., leaning), head movement, arm and hand gestures, and facial expressions which both modify the verbal message and affect the impression they convey.[39]

4.2. *Ryo's nonverbal behavior*

In Example (39), the one male, Ryo, in addition to smiling and nodding, changes posture and gestures frequently. The shifts in posture occur primarily when he is listening to Ann. They involve Ryo leaning forward, with his gaze fixed on the native speaker (see lines 2, 4, 6, 8 in Example 39). In Figure 7 (Picture a), we see him leaning forward as the native speaker displays her pierced ears.

When Ryo is speaking, he uses gestures, especially during his refusals. Lines 12, 14, 16, 18, 20 and 28 all involve gestures accompanying a refusal. This can be seen in Figure 7 (Picture b). Although the hand to the ear in the same line could be taken as reinforcing the message about pierced ears, the jerky, pulling motion with which Ryo tugs seems almost indicative of his linguistic struggle.

The nonverbal behavior associated with each of Ryo's linguistic refusals (including leaning back, line 12; head shake, line 14; and particularly the extension of his arm and the waving of his hand in front of his body, one or the other of which accompanies each refusal) reinforces and emphasizes the verbal message in the refusal. In fact, the gestures accompanying each of this non-native speaker's refusals are broad and emphatic, and the posture is exaggerated, as in Figure 7.

In addition to the gestures and actions that reinforce his refusal, Ryo's brief account of why he is refusing (line 22) is also accompanied by gestures. In this case, the non-native speaker's actions seem more to emphasize his difficulty in expressing himself than to reinforce the message. For instance, the stomp in line 22 (see Figure 8) accompanies a part of the utterance where Ryo indicates difficulty in expressing his idea with grimaces as well.[40] And thus, Ryo uses gestures and posture (with an occasional grimace not noted in the transcript) which

1. indicate his attention to his conversational partner (as a listener),
2. reinforce his (spoken) refusal, and
3. communicate his effort at producing a (spoken) message.

Picture a   Picture b

Figure 7: Ryo's posture

4.3. *Mie's nonverbal behavior*

The non-native speaker in Example (40), Mie, relies on many of the nonverbal resources employed by Ryo in Example (39). She uses a range of head movements, gestures, postures, and facial expressions that seem to perform a variety of functions. As with Ryo, Mie uses her posture to indicate attention when listening to Ann (line 2), at the

Picture a   Picture b   Picture c

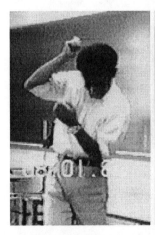  

Picture d   Picture e   Picture f

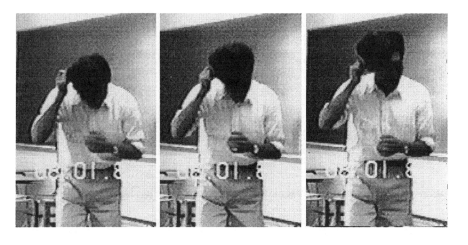

| Picture g | Picture h | Picture i |

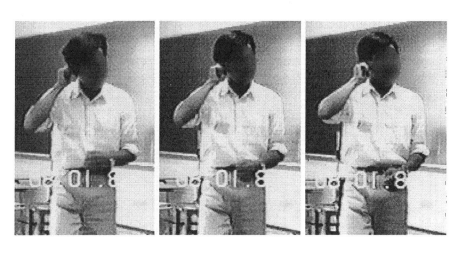

| Picture j | Picture k | Picture l |

Figure 8. Stomp

same time moving toward her (see Figure 9). In line 21, she leans forward and moves forward at a point where she seems not to have understood Ann (Pictures a and b). A careful look at Pictures a and b shows her leaning forward and, particularly in Picture a, craning her neck. At the same time, she turns her head so that one ear is directed toward the native speaker, conveying a strong impression of a listener attempting to understand.

As with Ryo, when speaking, Mie's gestures

a. reinforce the refusal itself (lines 6, 15, 17, 23) (see Figure 10 in which she waves as part of the refusal),
b. reinforce her reason for refusing (lines 8, 11) but, additionally, even before her first refusal,
c. telegraph a refusal nonverbally after the native speaker has expressed her offer but before the native speaker has stopped speaking (line 5).

The reinforcement that is seen in Figure 10 is particularly protracted as is clear from the sequence of pictures a-aa.

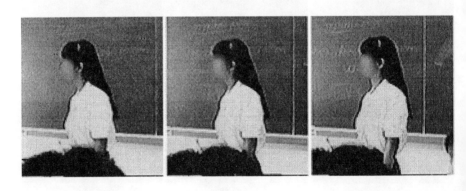

Picture a   Picture b   Picture c

Figure 9. Leaning

Unlike Ryo in Example (39), she also uses gestures which are not associated with refusing to reinforce her verbal message (line 8, hand to ear, pointing at TV; line 11, hand to ear) and perhaps to indicate that she is following the native speaker's message (line 3, pointing at TV). Also, unlike Ryo, Mie's gestures are not broad and emphatic, but rather are small and hesitant. This is reflected in lines 5-6, which describe nonverbal behavior that might be characterized as delicate and gracious. Finally, although not noted in the transcript, Mie's face is particularly mobile, with a wide range of expressions, from interested smile to concerned frown.

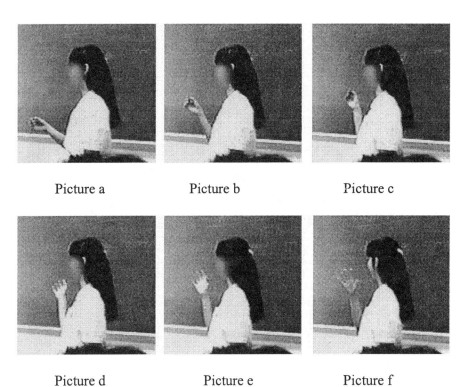

Picture a   Picture b   Picture c

Picture d   Picture e   Picture f

Picture g   Picture h   Picture i

Picture j   Picture k   Picture l

Picture m   Picture n   Picture o

Picture p   Picture q   Picture r

Picture s   Picture t   Picture u

Picture v   Picture w   Picture x

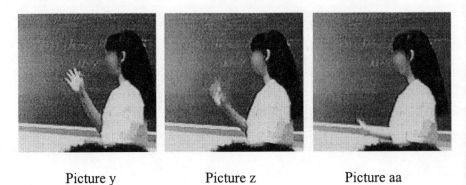

| Picture y | Picture z | Picture aa |

Figure 10. Hand wave

5. Comparison of nonverbal activity of the three non-native speakers

All three of the non-native speakers considered in this chapter employ nonverbal resources. Even Rie, the non-native speaker in Example (38) who gestured minimally, smiled relentlessly throughout the interaction. However, the resources adopted differ in quantity, quality (both type and manner of delivery), and function. Thus, the non-native speakers in Examples (39) and (40), Ryo and Mie, rely more heavily 1) on gestures that reinforce their linguistic message, 2) on posture and head movements that indicate involvement in the native speaker's message, and 3) on facial expressions that convey feelings about the interaction. At the same time, Ryo and Mie differ radically from one another in the manner in which they perform the gestures, head movements, postures, and facial expressions. They even differ somewhat in the range of functions which these behaviors perform.

Since, as Patterson (1994) has noted, high involvement behaviors such as those used by the non-native speakers in Examples (39) and (40) are associated with positive impression management, these two individuals may be conveying a more involved, and (thus perhaps more positive), personal impression to an American viewer, when compared with the non-native speaker in Example (38).[41]

6. Conclusion

While all three non-native speakers 1) use comparable language, 2) achieve their speech act objective (an effective refusal), and 3) avoid obvious linguistic or cross-cultural misunderstandings, the effects and impressions they impart are quite different.[42] In fact, an attempt to interpret these interactions and their effects based only on linguistic information would be incomplete, if not misleading. And it is only through the use of video that we have access to this window on their attempt to manage affective factors.

As we hope to have made clear from these data, understanding a complete speech act negotiation entails having access to the full event, including visual information. There are many aspects of a communicative event that may be enhanced or modified by access to nonverbal information. As Rosenfeld (1987:589) notes: "Given the considerable independent and interactive effects of the nonverbal channel, it is quite clear that both channels of communication must be integrated into a comprehensive theory of conversational structure and process."

Chapter 6
Pragmatic communication strategies

1. Introduction

In this chapter we will take a broader view of some of the behaviors of the non-native speakers reported in previous chapters, relating their use of interactional resources to their ability to communicate acceptably within their second language. To do this, we will look at a range of linguistic and nonlinguistic behaviors in terms of their potential role as pragmatic communication strategies.

Since the mid-1970s there has been a growing interest not only in non-native speakers' acquisition of target language grammatical forms, but in their development of communicative competence in the target language, where communicative competence refers to the internalized knowledge of the language user which results in the ability to produce and comprehend grammatically accurate and situationally appropriate utterances (Ellis 1994). A number of models have been developed to represent the types of knowledge necessary for communicative competence (Bachman 1990; Bachman and Palmer 1996; Canale 1983; Celce-Murcia, Dörnyei, and Thurrell 1995). Among their components these models usually include grammatical competence and some version of pragmatic competence, where grammatical competence is generally defined as knowledge of the language code — vocabulary, word formation, sentence formation, and pronunciation — as well as the ability to access that knowledge, and pragmatic competence refers to the linguistic and sociocultural knowledge necessary to perform speech acts such as greetings, requests, complaints, and refusals appropriately, along with the ability to access that knowledge.

Most models of communicative competence also posit a role for communication strategies, the mental resources used to compensate for problems in communication that result from inadequate linguistic or sociocultural knowledge. Communication strategies are usually included as part of a more general strategic competence component.

In the past 15 years a significant amount of research has been conducted on aspects of pragmatic competence (Blum-Kulka, House, and Kasper 1989; Gass and Neu 1996; Kasper and Blum-Kulka 1993; Kasper and Dahl 1991), and on communication strategies (Bialystok 1990; Færch and Kasper 1983a; Kasper and Kellerman 1997). However, despite the large body of emerging literature, pragmatic communication strategies have only begun to receive attention. In this chapter we look at second language pragmatic competence, as represented by the performance of a speech act in English by non-native speakers, and at the pragmatic communication strategies that these non-native speakers draw on when they run into difficulty. The first sections provide a brief background on communication strategies in general and pragmatic communication strategies in particular. We then go on to focus on questions of learner behavior exhibited in our data, identifying the goals that their behavior reflects and those behaviors that seem to function as communication strategies designed to help the non-native speakers achieve these goals.

1.1. *Communication strategies*

As already mentioned, communication strategies are the approaches that "learners use to overcome the inadequacies of their interlanguage resources" (Ellis 1994: 396). A number of theoretical approaches have been used to characterize communication strategies. However, many researchers agree with Færch and Kasper (1983a) that communication strategies are essentially a response to a communication problem (usually a linguistic one) and, to a lesser extent, that they are potentially conscious behaviors (behaviors employed consciously at least sometimes by some individuals). Bialystok (1990) presents the following definitions that had previously appeared in the second language literature:

> a systematic technique employed by a speaker to express his meaning when faced with some difficulty (Corder 1977)

a mutual attempt of two interlocutors to agree on a meaning in situations where requisite meaning structures are not shared (Tarone 1980)

potentially conscious plans for solving what to an individual presents itself as a problem in reaching a particular communicative goal (Færch and Kasper 1983b)

techniques of coping with difficulties in communicating in an imperfectly known second language (Stern 1983).

Bialystok goes on to point out three features that are common to definitions of communication strategies: 1) problematicity, 2) consciousness, and 3) intentionality. However, she also notes that each of these areas is replete with a lack of precision and, importantly, that none of these is unique to the concept of communication strategies.

With regard to (1), problematicity, she points out that communication strategies are "consistent with descriptions of language processing where no problem is perceived" (p. 146). In other words, strategic language use is not fundamentally different from nonstrategic language use in the underlying processes each calls upon for execution. With regard to (2), consciousness, her argument against the uniqueness of communication strategies relies on the fact that there is "universal dependence upon a small set of ...strategies" (p. 146) common to both children and adults in a wide range of circumstances. She claims that this contradicts the notion that consciousness is involved in the production of a communication strategy. Finally, she maintains with respect to (3), intentionality, that "the absence of a relation between choosing a specific strategy and solving a certain kind of problem contradicts the notion that communication strategies can be identified on the basis of intentionality" (p. 146). Strategic choice, she argues, can be identified on the basis of proficiency and cognitive sophistication rather than on the basis of selecting among strategies. In other words, learners do not intentionally select one strategy or the other with the goal of a predictable outcome; the strategies they select are based on linguistic and cognitive maturity.

We now turn from a discussion of the necessary characteristics of communication strategies to a discussion of the purposes that have been adopted in the investigation of communication strategies. Non-native speaker communication strategies are investigated for a variety of reasons, some of them complementary. In a discussion of different approaches to the study of communication strategies, Yule and Tarone (1997) mention a number of research agendas, including the following:

1. determine the psychological processes underlying second language acquisition and use
2. describe the forms observed in social interaction
3. compare the forms produced by a non-native speaker with those of a native speaker for insight into the learner's interlanguage, particularly as an aid to understanding why certain strategies are more or less effective in interaction and, relatedly, how the learner's strategies elicit relevant input from the native speaker
4. determine similarities between the communication strategies used by the learner in the L1 and in the L2
5. determine the potential effect of instruction of certain communication strategies on communication

Thus, the study of communication strategies is perceived to have value by researchers investigating a number of aspects of non-native speaker second language use.

Most of the research conducted on communication strategies has looked at the strategies used when a particular lexical item is unavailable. For example, some typical communication strategies for the lexical item *umbrella* in English or Japanese include paraphrase (e.g., "that thing that you open over your head to protect you from rain"); mime (e.g., gesture indicating the opening of an umbrella); foreignizing of a word (e.g., making an English word sound Japanese, as in /amburera/ for *umbrella*); and appeal for assistance (e.g., looking up the word in a dictionary, or asking a linguistically more knowledgeable speaker for the word).

These strategy types are appropriate primarily for communicating a problematic or unavailable lexical item. And in fact, little research has been done on the use of communication strategies in other areas of second language production. However, communication strategies may also have a role to play in discovering how pragmatically successful communication is achieved by non-native speakers with limited proficiency (as well as how and what types of pragmatic miscommunication may result from their choices).

1.2. *Pragmatic communication strategies*

Although most work on communication strategies has focused on non-native speaker utterances produced when there is a need to compensate for lexical problems, recently interest has focused on how non-native speakers deal with the complex interpersonal problems they face when they interact with native speakers. As Janney and Arndt (1992) observe,

> Many problems of intercultural communication arise from the difficulty of finding appropriate ways to signal feelings and attitudes to foreign partners....Even relatively simple misunderstandings are sometimes difficult to regulate in intercultural situations because the techniques and strategies of tact for resolving them are not fully shared by the partners (p. 21).

Janney and Arndt note that in intracultural communication, speakers from the same community share strategies for resolving the constant threats to face that arise even in everyday interactions. However, in intercultural communication, these resources are not shared. Different cultures have different emotive styles and strategies of interacting. As Janney and Arndt state, whereas "breakdowns in propositional communication often have little lasting effect on conversation,...breakdowns in emotive communication...can lead to serious intercultural misunderstandings" (p. 31).

Thus, it becomes a matter of some relevance to investigate the strategies used by non-native speakers in their attempt to maintain a positive relationship with a native speaker conversational partner, particularly when these non-native speakers are attempting to perform a potentially face-threatening act effectively.

Kasper (1997) discusses the notion of pragmatic communication strategies, specifically in terms of the production of speech acts by non-native speakers. Relying on the same model of speech production used by Færch and Kasper (1983a) in their discussion of communication strategies, Kasper defines the "problem" of producing pragmatically appropriate speech acts.

Kasper notes that while lexical problems and the communication strategies associated with them are concerned with propositional (semantic) accuracy, there are other types of problems that a non-native speaker may confront that result from a lack of linguistic or sociocultural knowledge. When performing speech acts such as requesting, apologizing, or refusing, speakers often face the problem of managing conflicting goals. In particular, they may need to balance the goal of effective performance of the act with that of establishment or maintenance of a positive relationship.

Although native speakers also confront similar problems, they have a large store of background knowledge as well as grammatical or pragmatic knowledge (which they share with other same-language speaker interlocutors), the latter often in the form of situationally appropriate patterns or routines, which they can call on quickly. Even advanced non-native speakers often do not possess the requisite situation-specific knowledge, and if they do, are unable to access appropriate routines on the spot.

In her discussion of pragmatic communication strategies used by non-native speakers to deal with the tension between effective performance of a speech act and maintenance of a cordial relationship, Kasper (1997) draws on the results of prior studies of speech acts. She argues that several behaviors set non-native speakers apart from native speakers of both the first language and the second language when they perform speech acts in the second language. Kasper proposes that these behaviors qualify as communication strategies. They include a) bluntness and b) verbosity. She also notes that non-native speakers may use their "non-nativeness" as an interactional resource to establish alignment with the native speaker. Kasper (personal communication) admits that there is no easy way to determine whether a particular pragmatic behavior is a new one or has been automatized through use and has been incorporated into the learner's pragmatic interlanguage. Thus, current criteria for identifying a behavior as a pragmatic communication strategy include linguistic deviation from both L1 and l2 norms and explicit or implicit indications of awareness of his/her status as a non-native speaker by the non-native speaker.

By bluntness or directness, Kasper refers to inappropriately direct acts. For example, the forms in Example (41) were produced by native speakers of Japanese role playing the part of a student asking to borrow a book from a lecturer who was a native speaker of English.

(41) From Tanaka (1988: 90)

    a) NNS: Can I borrow X?
    b) NNS: I'd like to borrow X.

On the other hand, native speakers of English who role played the student asking to borrow the book used the following forms:

(42) From Tanaka (1988: 90)

    a) NS: What I came to ask about was whether or not I could borrow X
    b) NS: I thought I might see if I could borrow X.

Thus, although the requests produced by the non-native speakers were clear and unambiguous, they were rather abrupt when contrasted with those of native speakers of English, which in this situation were less blunt by virtue of their less direct, more tentative nature.

Kasper's second communication strategy, a verbose or more explicit response, contrasts with a blunt or overly direct approach in that the non-native speaker provides an unnecessary amount of information. This can be illustrated by an example from a large corpus of written data collected by Edmondson and House (1991). When instructed to write a request asking a neighbor for a ride home, a native speaker of German gave the following response in English:

(43) From Edmondson and House (1991: 275)

> NNS: Good evening.   Perhaps you've already seen me
>   once. We're living in the same street. You know,
>   my bus has just left, and as I noticed that you have
>   come by car I was going to ask you whether you
>   could give me a lift.

Given the same instructions, a native speaker of British English
produced the request in Example (44):

(44) From Edmondson and House (1991: 276)

> NS: Excuse me, could you give me a lift home?

Here the non-native speaker supplies much more information than
the native speaker (44 words versus 9 words), who in this situation
resorts to a brief conventional indirect request, preceded by an
alerter, *excuse me*.

In addition to bluntness and verbosity, a number of studies of
non-native speaker interactions with native speakers have also described typically non-native speaker behaviors that serve to establish
social ties with the native speakers. These include, for example,
seeking agreement (Fiksdal 1990), establishing a common task orientation (Janney and Arndt 1992), or using admission of incompetence as a way of negotiating support (Aston 1993).

Thus, Kasper claims that data from prior research indicate that
non-native speakers use certain linguistic and interpersonal behaviors as strategies to compensate for their lack of the sociocultural
and pragmalinguistic knowledge and ability needed to perform effective and/or supportive speech acts appropriately. Information on
learner use of communication strategies in the performance of face-
threatening speech acts may provide further insight into the relative
importance of the success (or lack of success) of an act versus the
maintenance of a relationship for particular learners. It may also
reveal interactional areas that the learner is aware of and is at some
level attending to.

2. Questions

In analyzing our refusal data from the theoretical perspective of communication strategies, we take as a point of departure Kasper's definition of the pragmatic problem of performing appropriate speech acts clearly, that is, the problem of performing a speech act both effectively and, at the same time, supportively. This conception was the basis for formulating the following questions and later for interpreting the non-native speakers' behavior as possible communication strategies.

1. In refusal interactions with native speakers of English, did the native speakers of Japanese speaking English
   a. yield to face/solidarity concerns by abandoning the refusal and accepting? Or
   b. persist in a Nonaccept of the original initiating act?
2. If the non-native speakers persisted in a Nonaccept, was their behavior oriented exclusively to refusal, or was it also oriented to face-saving or solidarity-building concerns?
3. Did non-native speakers engaged in a Nonaccept employ non-native speaker-specific strategies for effective refusal or face saving/solidarity building? If so, what were they?

3. General results

The initial analysis of outcomes and semantic formulas discussed in Chapter Two lays the groundwork for responding to the questions posed above.

3.1. *Question one: Outcomes*

To answer question one, whether the refuser emphasized face concerns and, ultimately, accepted the initiating act or whether the refuser persisted with non-acceptance, the outcome of each interaction was examined.

Willingness to abandon the refusal and accept a request, invitation, offer, or suggestion varied according to the eliciting act and the situation. An inspection of the data revealed that in 8 out of 23 of the role play situations in which no physical danger or discomfort was involved and no obligation would be violated (e.g., a suggestion of a punk haircut or a request to make a speech at church), the non-native speakers resolved the conflict by accepting the request, invitation, offer, or suggestion even after initially refusing. So, in a sense, they chose to abandon their refusal, thus avoiding the problems inherent in disappointing their host (although occasionally they attempted to have some say in how the requested act was carried out).[43]

On the other hand, in instances in which acceptance involved the possibility of serious discomfort or harm, or violation of an obligation, the non-native speakers in the study remained firm in their non-acceptance of the original request, invitation, offer, or suggestion. These included a request by a stranger to enter the host family home, an invitation to go skydiving, and an offer of ear piercing.

Thus, in a number of cases, the refusal was abandoned. However, in the remaining situations, the non-native speaker refused to go along with the native speaker's request, invitation, offer, or suggestion, thereby maintaining the original refusal.

3.2. *Question two: Refusal orientation*

This leads to question two. In those situations in which the outcome was not acceptance, did the non-native speaker direct his/her efforts primarily to performing an effective refusal? Or, was an orientation to face saving or solidarity detectable?

In most instances in which the outcome of the interaction was non-acceptance, the non-native speakers stuck closely to clear refusal formulas – direct refusals such as "no" or "I can't," with frequent excuses and occasional expressions of regret. When the native speaker persisted, they recycled the direct refusal, excuse, and/or regret until the refusal was accepted. In these interactions, although regret was sometimes expressed and reasons proffered, the primary orientation was usually clearly toward an effective refusal.

On the other hand, evidence of an orientation toward relationship goals was revealed in the use of additional semantic formulas such as alternatives, and in particular in their content. In slightly fewer than half the role plays, after expressing one or more of the basic semantic formulas discussed above, the non-native speaker branched out and attempted more complex negotiations involving alternatives.[44] Alternatives can vary widely as to content, and the content of the alternatives in the data often differed greatly not only with respect to the initiating act and the situation surrounding it, but also to the extent that concern for the native speaker was demonstrated. Some of the different types of alternatives found in the data are listed below:

1. Proposal of an alternative activity to the one suggested by the native speaker (to be arranged in some cases by the native speaker, in others, by the non-native speaker)
2. Suggestion as to how the native speaker could solve a problem resulting from the refusal, without a corresponding offer of help
3. Offer to help the native speaker in solving a problem resulting from the refusal, without granting the original request.

The content of these alternatives indicates different degrees of supportive involvement, evidencing varying concern with the effect of the alternative on the relationship. Thus, although non-native speakers ended up not accepting the native speaker's original request, etc., they occasionally involved themselves in the native speaker's problems and sometimes committed themselves to alternative activities involving the native speaker.

The strongest orientation to the relationship with the native speaker was demonstrated in situations in which the non-native speaker continued to show concern for the native speaker and the relationship even after the refusal had been accepted. In one role play, in which the native speaker hostess had invited the non-native speaker to a party with drugs, after much discussion on the dangers of drugs, the native speaker stopped trying to convince the non-native speaker to come along to the party with her and started to leave. If a refusal orientation were the primary goal of the non-native speaker, one would expect the interaction to end at that point. But in spite of the native speaker host's capitulation, the non-native speaker did not allow the interaction to come to a close. An excerpt is given in Example (45).

(45) Drugs situation

> (The non-native speaker's reaction to the native speaker's decision to leave without him is highlighted in **boldface**.)

> NS: ok I'm gonna go I'll see you later ok Hidetaki?
>   ok I'll see you tomorrow
>   [
> NNS: unn huh?
>   **I only?**=
> NS: =sayonara
> NNS: (.) **I onl- uh only I? are here? you go?**
> NS: what can I do. I want to go to this party. I uh I told
>   my friends that I would meet you that they would
>   meet you at this party
> NNS: **ok you don't you don't take**
>   [
> NS: I tell you what, we'll just go
>   for a few minutes how's that, do you want to go for
>   just a few minutes? ok?
> NNS: **yes. but you don't take you won't take that drug?**
> NS: ((sighs)) ok I won't

Such concern goes beyond the requirements of a linguistically appropriate refusal and a polite attempt to save face.[45]

Thus, different levels of concern regarding the relationship with the native speaker are detectable in the responses used by non-native speakers in negotiating a non-acceptance. They extend from a clear concentration on the achievement of an effective refusal, as evidenced in the recycling of direct refusals, reasons, and regrets, to demonstration of concern for the native speaker, as evidenced by the content of some alternatives, to explicit attention to the relationship even after an effective refusal was achieved.

The non-native speakers' choice of semantic formulas and content shows that non-native speakers who elect not to accept a native speaker's request may display different degrees of concern for the effectiveness of the refusal and the maintenance of the relationship.[46] This leads to the question of whether there are non-native speaker behavioral resources that may enable the learners to achieve their goals despite a significant lack of pragmatic competence in the second language.

3.3. *Question three: Strategies*

In response to question three concerning the pragmatic strategies specific to non-native speakers when refusing, the investigation again focuses on those instances in which the non-native speaker achieved an outcome other than acceptance (e.g., a refusal or a compromise that did not involve agreeing to the original request). It concentrates on identifying linguistic and nonlinguistic behaviors in these interactions that seem in some way particular to non-native speakers, and that indicate attention to the goals of achieving a refusal in the face of resistance and/or mitigating the effect of the act or conciliating the relationship.

We identified five behaviors that seemed to be operating as communication strategies. The next section is devoted to an extensive discussion of these behaviors.

4. Japanese pragmatic communication strategies

A search of the data for pragmatic strategies which might be particular to non-native speakers revealed five types of behavior that met the criteria.

The proposed pragmatic communication strategies include the following:

1. Bluntness (or directness)
2. Indications of linguistic or sociocultural inadequacy
   a. Explicit reference to lack of (sociocultural) knowledge

      b. Explicit reference to lack of linguistic ability
      c. Request for explanation of known term
      d. Nonverbal demonstration of production difficulty
3. Use of the L1
4. Sequential shifts (in attention to goal, choice of semantic formula, and choice of content of excuses or alternatives)
5. Nonverbal expressions of affect

Two of these types corresponded to behaviors mentioned by Kasper (1997): 1) bluntness and 2) a calling of attention to aspects of the speaker's linguistic or sociocultural inadequacy, which Kasper, citing Aston (1993), refers to as an instance of a strategy that not only compensates for lack of common ground, but exploits the non-native speaker's differences as a resource for "negotiating solidarity and support" (p. 353). Another pragmatic strategy, noted by Kasper, volubility (or explicitness), was not observed.[47] Each of the proposed strategy types will be discussed briefly with examples from our data.

4.1. *Bluntness*

As Kasper has noted, the first communication strategy, bluntness, is frequently associated with non-native speaker speech acts. This may result from use of, for instance, an inappropriately direct semantic formula or a socioculturally inappropriate excuse. Bluntness usually reflects an orientation to the effective performance of the act. Kasper notes that while this maintaining of the speech act goal without marking the act for politeness may result from the non-native speaker's processing limitations, it frequently represents a choice, a strategy of "modality reduction" (p. 350).

    As mentioned above, non-native speakers often used a direct semantic formula (e.g., "no," "I can't") to express their refusal.[48] In the majority of cases, these direct refusals were accompanied by other semantic formulas, such as a reason and/or a statement of regret, which softened the effect. However, in several instances, the non-native speaker relied exclusively on repetition of a direct refusal, as in Example (46), in which the native speaker of English host is inviting the non-native speaker visitor to go skydiving. (The relevant non-native speaker linguistic contributions are highlighted in **boldface**.)

(46) Skydiving situation
       (HS refers to head shake; NODS, to head nods)

     NS: you will go skydiving
     NNS: **ah no**
     NS: no?
     NNS: NODS
     NS: no no what ((laughs)) no you don't like to skydive?
     NNS: NODS **skydiving** HS **no**
     NS: oh are y- do you not like to skydive? you do not like to skydive?
     NNS: **no**
     NS: no? ok ohh it's very fun have you tried it before?
     NNS: HS **no**
     NS: we could teach you how
     NNS: HS **no**
     NS: no
     NNS: NODS
     NS: are you sure?
     NNS: eh?
     NS: are you sure?
     NNS: yes

In this example, the native speaker of Japanese runs little risk of having his refusal misunderstood. He even emphasizes his "no"s with head shakes. Several non-native speakers took a similar approach, reiterating their refusal; however, most provided reasons, sometimes with rather direct content (e.g., "it's horrible").

In these instances, unambiguous performance of the refusal seemed to be the dominant goal, and directness played a part in achieving it.

4.2. *Indications of linguistic or sociocultural inadequacy*

The second communication strategy identified in the data involved non-native speakers drawing attention to some aspect of their non-nativeness in negotiating their response. As mentioned above, Kasper comments that non-native speakers may use their non-nativeness to negotiate solidarity or solicit support from the native speaker. In the data reported on in this book, the drawing of attention to non-nativeness seemed to function primarily to emphasize the non-native speakers' linguistic or sociocultural limitations. As will be discussed below, learners' indications of their linguistic and sociocultural inadequacy may have acted to create a social bond, but most obviously, it made salient to the native speakers how the non-native speakers' linguistic deficiencies impeded their ability to express their intent. Varonis and Gass (1985a) similarly noted the willingness of low proficiency non-native speakers (particularly those in a learning setting) to admit to language deficiencies.

The non-native speakers resorted to the following ways of calling attention to their lack of native-like competence:

1. reference to their lack of sociocultural knowledge
2. reference to their lack of linguistic knowledge
3. requests for explanations of terms with which they were already familiar
4. nonverbal demonstration of their production difficulty

In attempting to refuse, the non-native speaker occasionally mentioned explicitly a lack of knowledge about how to behave under the circumstances as a reason for not complying with a request. In Example (47), the non-native speaker has opened the door to a stranger, who claims to be the host's cousin. The host is out and the stranger is asking to be admitted.

(47) Cousin situation

> NNS: ah no wait wait I'm a guest to uh this home the- I can't uh I don't uh uh um I can't **I don't know what uh I do this situation then** eh

Non-native speakers also commented on their lack of linguistic ability. In the situations where their linguistic abilities were being called on, their inadequate knowledge of English was explicitly invoked as a reason for not complying with a request to speak to the host's church group, as in Example (48). Here the native speaker has just informed the non-native speaker that she is expected to give a speech at the native speaker's church that day:

(48) Speech at church situation

      NNS: **I can I cannot** (uh) ((tsk))
      NS: I cannot
      NNS: **speak English**

      NS: ohh (.) so y-
                   [
      NNS: **very little**

In addition to these explicit expressions of lack of competence, the non-native speakers also displayed their linguistic inability less directly, occasionally under suspect conditions. While requests for clarification are usually considered as part of negotiation of meaning, not part of the refusal process itself, Bardovi-Harlig and Hartford (1991) have reported that non-native speakers in college counseling sessions who are trying to reject the advice of an advisor sometimes use requests for explanations or repetitions as an avoidance strategy. In the data under study, this strategy also occurs, as shown in Chapter Two. Example (7) from Chapter Two, reprinted below, illustrates such a use of a request for clarification. The non-native speaker has just been informed that the family plans to go skydiving that day.

(49) Skydiving situation

      NNS: **what is**
      NS: what is skydiving

As noted in Chapter Two, in this example, the non-native speaker asks the host to explain skydiving, despite the fact that she had already had the term clarified before the role play. This results in a helpful response, as the term is once again explained to her. It also gives the non-native speaker an opportunity to react to the explanation, thus signaling her feelings without initially articulating a direct refusal.

Another indirect means of indicating linguistic inadequacy mentioned briefly in Chapter Two and discussed at greater length in Chapter Five was nonverbal resources. In several instances non-native speakers displayed their linguistic difficulty nonverbally (e.g., through facial expressions, hands cupped to ears), thus conveying their lack of linguistic skill independently of the semantic formulas they employed. Line 22 of Example (39) in Chapter Five is reproduced below. As discussed in Chapter Five, the non-native speaker's actions accompanying this utterance illustrate how he communicated production difficulty nonverbally.

(50) Pierced ears situation

> NNS: ah I don't want to be pierced   (.)   my ears
>   HAND TO EAR ----------------------------
>   JERKY MOTION   STOMP

The non-native speaker pulls at his ears and scrunches up his face as he speaks, giving the impression that he is pulling out the words, and then stomps after successfully producing the first segment of the phrase.

Non-native speakers' emphasis on their incompetence may have served in the data to diminish the threat of the refusal, or to indicate the refuser's need for help, or even to buy time. In most (but not all) cases, native speakers responded to a non-native speaker's reference to communication problems with a supportive orientation to the refuser's difficulty.

4.3. *Use of the L1*

A third communication strategy identified in the data was reliance on the first language (in this case, Japanese) semantic formulas. Use of the native language as a solution to a lack of pragmatic knowledge, rather than as part of the learner's pragmatic competence in the second language, is difficult to identify. However, there are several indications in the data that learners were aware of the possibility of relying on native language refusal formulas and that they were reluctant to use certain semantic formulas that they might ordinarily have used in their first language, but which they recognized as unusual or marked.

One hint of this awareness and reluctance to transfer a native language behavior is a total absence in the data of a common Japanese refusal behavior, that of inhaling through the mouth. None of the Japanese non-native speakers in the data relied on this means of signaling a refusal. The absence of this particular behavior may indicate that learners were mindful of its uniqueness to Japanese and made an active choice not to transfer (cf. Kellerman 1979 for a similar argument regarding transfer).

On the other hand, there are behaviors which have been identified in Japanese refusal data but not in American refusal data, and which are not as obviously culture-specific as that of oral inhalation. For instance, Beebe, Takahashi and Uliss-Weltz (1990) noted that Japanese often employed expressions of empathy when refusing, but the American subjects never did. In the extended interaction discussed in detail in Chapter Three and summarized below, one of the non-native speakers became embroiled in a long interaction with the native speaker when he refused to admit her to the house, and she kept insisting that she should be allowed to enter. After producing a number of different semantic formulas, the non-native speaker finally expressed empathy for the native speaker's situation. This was not a strategy which the non-native speaker employed in his initial refusal. In fact, it was not until the native speaker had recycled her request four times that the non-native speaker responded with empathy. Thus, the non-native speaker exhibited apparent reluctance to rely on some less common first language semantic formulas until other more general semantic formulas proved inadequate in achieving either an effective refusal or a cordial supportive interaction.

4.4. *Sequential shifts in goal, semantic formula, or content*

Another communication strategy that we identified was noticeable sequential shifts in goal, semantic formula, or content. These occurred when a non-native speaker ran into real trouble — for instance, a complex linguistic misunderstanding or the unintentional giving of offense — and needed to re-establish the refusal or work to achieve a relational goal. Such occurrences were rare, but when they did take place, they offered an interesting window onto the process of strategy selection. Thus, in the extended refusal sequence discussed in Chapter Three, the non-native speaker tried direct *no*, statement of regret, several different reasons, two alternatives, and, finally empathy. The result is a wealth of semantic formulas and content. See Table Three for a summary. The non-native speaker's semantic formulas are in boldface. Explanatory material, nonverbal reactions, or alternative interpretations are included in parentheses.

Table 3.   Summary of Native Speaker-Non-Native Speaker Refusal Sequence

Native Speaker	Non-Native Speaker
1. Greetings (Background: Reasons for Request)	
I REQUEST 1	
	a. **Direct "no"**
	b. **Reason a**–guest
	c. **Reason b**–don't know what to do
2. Request for Clarif of Reason b	
	Clarification of Reason b
3. Rejection of Reason b	
	Repetition of **Reason b** (or begin Reason c)

4. Repetition of Rejection of Reason b

Reason c – first time to meet (=I don't know you)

5. Response to Reason c
   (=Introduction of Self)

   a. Reason for Altern. 1
   b. **Altern 1**–Wait in car

6. (Reaction =Rejection of Alt 1)
   Reason for React/Reject

   Restatement of **Reason c**

7. Statement of Refusal Implication

   Restatement of **Reason c+**

8. a. Challenge (=Rejection of Reason c)
   b. Reason for Rejection
   c. Statement of Refusal Implication
   d. (Reaction)

   a. **Reason d**–statement of responsibility
   b. **Negative Ability**

9 Challenge (=Rejection of Reason d)

   Denial

10. a. Complaint

II   b. REQUEST 2

   c. Reason for Request
   d. Repetition of Request

   a. **Regret**
   b. **Reason e**–cannot decide

III

11. REQUEST 3 (2x)

   Alternative 2–look for neighbor's house

12. a. Request for Inform./Clarification re Alt 2
    b. Complaint

   a. Apology

| | b. Response to Request for Information/ Clarif |

13.Request for Confirmation

Confirmation

14.(Reaction)

Elaboration of Response to Request for Confirmation

15.a. (Sarcastic) Request for Clarification
   b. Reason for Request for Clarification

(Sincere) Response to Request for Clarification

16.(Sarcastic) Thanks

(Sincere) Acknowledgment

---

17.   a.   Summary of Situation
         (=Complaint at Alt 2)
         (=Reason to Reject Alt 2)

IV   b. REQUEST 4 (2x)
     c. Reason for Request

Acknowledgment

18.Confirmation

Empathy Expression

19.Confirmation

Empathy Expression

20.Reason for Request

Acknowledgment

---

21 REQUEST 5

Reasons e and b

22.a. (Reaction)
    b. Acceptance of Refusal
    c. Complaint/Farewell

As mentioned in Chapter Three, this non-native speaker's approach is in line with previous descriptions of Japanese refusals in English. However, the interaction is noteworthy for his unfortunate choice of content for the alternatives, which elicited a hostile reaction from the native speaker, as well as for the variety of semantic formulas (direct *no*, reasons, regret, alternatives, empathy) and content (five reasons, two alternatives) employed in dealing with the native speaker's responses.

The few cases in which non-native speakers ran into serious difficulty involved the most fluent participants — perhaps either because their more obvious fluency led the native speaker to negotiate more and not to accept an initial *no* or because these non-native speakers attempted more sophisticated problem resolution or relationship management. On the other hand, many of the more fluent non-native speakers did not adjust their strategies when faced with a persistent native speaker. Like the lower proficiency participants, they relied on an "adherence to refusal" strategy — a direct refusal, a single reason (or excuse), and/or a statement of regret. It may be that non-native speakers' reliance on a few semantic formulas in the second language allows them to avoid the problems that can result from venturing into the use of forms the effect of which they are less familiar with. Bardovi-Harlig (1998) has pointed out the important relationship between pragmatics and grammatical knowledge. Specifically, she notes that a prerequisite to appropriate pragmatic use is appropriate grammatical knowledge. The example that she provides is the use of *will* in English as opposed to a more softened and tentative version of the future, as in "I was going to x". It is established that learners learn core meanings before extensions (Andersen and Shirai 1996; Gass and Ard 1984). As Bardovi-Harlig notes "we cannot expect pragmatic extension of tense-mood-aspect forms until the core deictic meanings have been acquired" (p. 18).

It can be argued that a shifting in goals, semantic formulas, and content may occur in native speaker production of face-threatening acts such as refusal if the interlocutor becomes upset. However, since native speakers have access to a wide range of appropriate semantic formulas and content, inappropriate alternatives are much less likely to occur; and when they do occur, native speakers have a range of culture-specific responses at the tip of their tongue, the consequences of which can be predicted with some certainty.

4.5. *Nonverbal expressions of affect*

A final means of affecting the refusal was through nonverbal behavior. Nonverbal messages can have a profound effect on speakers' success both at conveying their refusal and at lessening its dis-
ruptive effect. The non-native speakers in this study occasionally
accompanied their refusals by laughter or by gestures or facial expressions which were judged by observers to have the purpose of
modifying or mitigating the act they were performing. Use of gestures as communication strategies has also been suggested by Gullberg (1998) and Kita (1993) (see also Chapter Five, where we suggested that a gamut of nonverbal behaviors may be used to modify
the effect of a refusal).

Although it is not clear that these nonverbal behaviors qualify as
communication strategies, there are indications that many are indeed
employed as communication strategies. Without further data, it is
difficult to determine whether the nonverbal conduct represented an
aspect of an individual's personality or was adopted or emphasized
specifically to cope with the problems encountered because of inadequate knowledge of the target culture or language or lack of access to appropriate routines. We mention these behaviors because
they too had a definite effect on the refusal and should be investigated in future research on pragmatic strategies.

5. Conclusion

In summary, we have claimed that the native speakers of Japanese
performing refusals in this study resorted to a number of pragmatic
communication strategies to make up for their deficiencies in pragmalinguistic and sociocultural knowledge and ability. They used
these communication strategies in attaining different goals — some,
primarily for establishing solidarity with the native speaker; some,
primarily for achieving the refusal; and some, serving both purposes.

The resources that these native speakers of Japanese drew on are
of interest because 1) they may reflect general strategies used by
non-native speakers from various cultures and 2) they may have a
role to play in the acquisition of pragmatic competence.

Since two of the behaviors found in the data — bluntness and reliance on non-nativeness — have already been mentioned by Kasper, it would appear that these at least occur cross-linguistically. An important question is how they are manifested by and how they vary among learners of different first languages. Two other categories — use of the first language and noticeable shifts in goal, semantic formula, or content — have each received attention in second language acquisition research, although not in terms of pragmatic communication strategies. Whether they share the generality of bluntness and reliance on non-nativeness has yet to be determined.

The second suggestion, that these communication strategies may be instrumental in acquisition of pragmatic competence, extends claims about the possible role of communication strategies in second language acquisition. Research by Gass (1997), Kasper and Kellerman (1997), and Long (1996) with specific regard to communication strategies, is of interest since they argue that the mechanisms used to keep conversations going result in the possibility of the greater availability to L2 learners of comprehensible input. This research area is also of potential value when considering the role of output (Swain 1985, 1995; Swain and Lapkin 1995, 1998), as these mechanisms afford an opportunity for feedback on learners' solutions to their communication problem (Kasper and Kellerman 1997) (see Chapter Eight, where these concepts will be discussed in greater detail). Thus, communication strategies can be seen to play a role in second language acquisition theories which focus on the importance of input, output, and feedback. It takes little imagination to extend the second of these claims — that they provide feedback — to pragmatic communication strategies. Clearly, the non-native speakers in the data discussed here were strongly influenced by the face-to-face feedback they received.

In addition, although they were not equally successful, a number of these communication strategies served to establish cordial relationships despite the problems posed by performance of a potentially face-threatening speech act, thus laying the groundwork for future interactions in which face-threatening acts could perhaps be negotiated with increasing trust.

Chapter 7
Searching for common ground

1. Conversational expectations

In previous chapters we have dealt with a number of areas of refusals, focusing for the large part on microanalyses of the exchange. This chapter is a departure in that we analyze the exchange from a global perspective focusing on how participants negotiate their way through a refusal and how they regain their footing when they appear to be going in different directions. We relate the need for negotiation to language specific and culture specific expectations that one has prior to performing, in this case, the speech act of refusal.

It has been well established by researchers such as Gumperz (1982) and Tannen (1984, 1990, 1993) that speakers of the same language enter into interactions with expectations about the nature of the interaction and how the interaction will proceed, and that they interpret the interaction and evaluate their fellow interactants in light of these expectations.[49] Expectations arise *inter alia* from prior knowledge and experiences. As Tannen (1993:15) notes, "As soon as we measure a new perception against what we know of the world from prior experience, we are dealing with expectations." Conflicting or mismatched expectations about how an interaction will develop may affect these interpretations and evaluations, ultimately influencing the smooth (or, in some instances, not so smooth) evolution of the event.

This notion of conflicting conversational expectations can be exemplified through an episode from the Monty Python movie "The Life of Brian." In the relevant scene, Brian, the protagonist, is hurriedly trying to buy a beard in an outdoor bazaar. He approaches the vendor and asks how much the beard is. The vendor quotes a specific price and Brian agrees to the price. The vendor, participating in a transaction in which bargaining is expected, is offended and refuses to sell without the expected bargaining process. He even attempts to coach Brian by telling him the specific linguistic forms which are supposed to be supplied by the buyer in this negotiation. Patiently, the vendor models an appropriate response to the quoted price of 10 shekels: "No it's not worth 10 shekels, you're supposed to argue, '10 for that, you must be mad'." In other words, like the vendor anticipating bargaining and Brian not operating in the framework of a bargaining encounter, speakers come to an interaction with expectations of the nature of the encounter and of the range of both requisite and possible moves within the encounter. And, as we show in this chapter, deviations from the expected can cause problems.

When the interaction is cross-cultural, the range of responses anticipated by individual participants may vary considerably (as has been shown by Gumperz 1982). In particular, research on cross-cultural speech acts by Beebe, Takahashi, and Uliss-Weltz (1990) and by members of the Cross-Cultural Speech Act Realization Project (see Blum-Kulka, House, and Kasper 1989) indicates that speakers from different cultures frequently conform to different patterns in the choice and content of semantic strategies involved in carrying out familiar speech acts. Thus, speakers from different cultures engage in speech act situations with often differing culturally conditioned expectations regarding the unfolding of the interaction.

In a case in which Speaker B is not only from a different culture than Speaker A, but is not a proficient speaker of A's language, it is to be anticipated that the expectations (whether local or global) of both speakers of the paths along which the interaction may progress will at least to some extent not be met.

Gass and Varonis (1985) noted a similar phenomenon in task-based activities. In their study non-native speakers were paired with the task of describing and drawing a picture. What they noted was the way that expectations of conversational content often led one speaker (the describer) to move the conversation along according to those expectations. "The describer has a more limited set of expectations of what the drawer can say since the drawer is bound by what the describer has already said. When the drawer's response appears to be outside of the range of the describer's expectations, the describer has the responsibility of bringing the drawer back on track" (p. 158).

Before turning to our data on refusals, we present data reported in Houck and Gass (in press) in which a disequilibrium or a "loss of footing" occurred at the beginning of a conversation as a result of differing expectations of how conversations of this specific type should unfold. We present these data to corroborate our own data of the significance of differing conversational structures.

The data we report here consist of conversations by pairs of graduate students in an American university in Japan. The pair that we focus on in this section consists of two women, one a native speaker of Japanese and the other a native speaker of English. The discussion was in English.

Both participants were enrolled in a course on second language acquisition, one of the last courses needed to complete their two-year degree program. In the data of concern here, the participants were involved in an open task (similar to others they had done in pairs or groups previously in the course), in which they had to evaluate and discuss concepts dealt with during the course. This particular task (adapted from a task developed by Rod Ellis, personal communication) required participants to evaluate Bley-Vroman's (1987) statements regarding the applicability of 10 characteristics to 1) second language acquisition, 2) first language acquisition and/or 3) general skill learning. Participants were instructed to consider each characteristic and determine to which of these three categories it applied. The data were collected toward the end of the semester.

For the purposes of demonstrating conversational disequilibrium, we have isolated one segment which illustrates the development and resolution of an uncomfortable moment, looking at it from the perspective of the non-native speaker of English.

The native Japanese speaker was in her mid 20s and was relatively fluent in English with a two-year old TOEFL score of 600. Both as a child and as an adult she had had considerable experience living in other countries, including a total of seven years in the U.S. The native speaker of English was in her late 30s and had also had considerable experience living in other cultures, including France, Israel, and Japan, where, at the time of data collection, she had been residing for nine years.

The part of the data that we will focus on comes at the very beginning of the interaction. The researcher has just left the room, and the native speaker of English starts with the utterance in Example (51).

(51) From Houck and Gass (in press)

> NS: okay so we're just gonna give our opinions about these, uhm do you have an overall opinion?

The NNS responds by repeating:

> NNS: do I have a overall (one)? uhm

At this point there is a longish pause accompanied by a movement of the non-native speaker's head, with her gaze shifting from the task sheet in front of her to her interlocutor. This movement culminates in a big smile, which she described in retrospective comments as sarcastic. The volume of her voice is low in comparison with the volume in later portions of this situation. The non-native speaker's response represents an uncomfortable moment, as evidenced by her pause, her repetition of the native speaker's previous utterance with rising intonation, her lowered volume, her unexpected body movement (posture shift, gaze, and facial expression), and her hesitation marker *uhm*.

The non smooth flowing nature of this opening was remarked on by other native speakers of Japanese who viewed the videotape and by the non-native speaker herself, who, after watching the taped interaction, stated that she was not certain what the native speaker was getting at with her question, and that this generalized confusion was the source of her question and nonverbal reaction. What is particularly interesting is that looking at the form of the discourse, one could also analyze the non-native speaker's repetition ("do I have a overall (one)?") as a "language" problem, where, for example, the non-native speaker did not know the meaning of the word "overall." In fact, much of the work within the input/interaction paradigm (see Gass 1997; Long 1980, 1981, 1983a, 1983b, 1996) in the field of second language acquisition would come to precisely that conclusion. However, if one takes a more global look at the situation, including the non-native speaker's linguistic background and proficiency, her retrospective comments, and her performance in other parts of the discourse, one can easily become convinced that the problem is a global discourse one and not a local linguistic one.

Why should such a simple opening pose difficulties to a high proficiency non-native speaker of English? On the face of it, the native speaker's opening remark and question seem innocuous enough, but perhaps that is because we are considering it from an English discourse perspective. Watanabe (1993) sheds some light on this particular issue. Her research examines native speaker discourse in groups of Americans and Japanese. Her data-base, comparable to ours, consists of an open task in which groups of same language speakers respond to open-ended questions such as "Why did you decide to learn Japanese" or "Why did you decide to study abroad?" Watanabe identified linguistic features in her data which she determined to be signaling framing differences between the two groups. The observations relevant to this section involve the opening of a task-oriented interaction.

According to Watanabe, the main difference between the openings of the Japanese groups and those of the American groups was the time required to "get into" the heart of the discussion. For the Americans, "okay" was a common opener, after which they launched right in, much as our English native speaker (American) did when she said "okay so we're just gonna give our opinions about these uhm do you have an overall opinion?" An example from one of Watanabe's American openings is given in Example (52).

(52) From Watanabe (1993: 182)

    Beth: Okay::=
    Mike: =So, Beth why did you decide to learn Japanese.
                          [
    Sean: Why.

Japanese, on the other hand, focused more on procedures for conducting their discussion. For example, the Japanese talked about the order of turns and how they would go about discussing the various topics. The following example is a translation of a typical Japanese negotiation at the beginning of a session.

(53) From Watanabe (1993: 184-185)

Yasuo:	Let's see as you see, uhm, basically we'll follow the number=
Keiko:	That's right. Number one, number two, and= =[
Fumiko:	H=h=h=h.
Keiko:	=number three.
Yasuo:	Hm. It's easy to get in.=
Keiko:	=That's right. Then..well, the top one, each one of us has to talk in turn, I wonder=
Fumiko:	=That is so.=
Yasuo:	=That's right…following numbers, how are we going to do…
Ikuo:	Ladies first.=
Fumiko:	=Please.
Yasuo:	=Oh, that sounds good.=
Fumiko:	[laugh] =[
Keiko:	[laugh]
Keiko:	Then, from the younger one. [laugh] [[
Fumiko:	Please [laugh]
Fumiko:	No, no. Big sister. [laugh]
Keiko:	What?
Ikuo:	It doesn't matter, does it.
Keiko:	As you see, [Keiko takes turn]

Thus, we are claiming on the basis of our data, as well as comments by the Japanese participant and other Japanese viewers, that an uncomfortable moment, what we earlier referred to as disequilibrium, occurred at the beginning of the discourse. Specifically, it appears that the native speaker's opening ("okay," followed soon thereafter by a question) caused the non-native speaker to lose her "conversational footing," inasmuch as the opening was unexpected, given her own discourse framework.[50]

We return to a brief discussion of refusal interactions and conclude with an explanation of the strategies used by native speakers with non-native speakers of limited proficiency which serve to orient the structure and content of the refusal interaction.

2. Refusal structure

Most refusal sequences in Japanese and English begin with Person A communicating, for example, a suggestion, invitation, offer, or request, and person B, when recognizing A's intention, responding, for instance, with one or more semantic formulas for refusal, postponement, or proposal of alternative (as discussed in Chapter One). As has been discussed in previous chapters, the frequency of occurrence of particular responses (i.e., particular semantic formulas or particular semantic content) may vary across cultures.

Depending on the semantic formulas and content employed by the refuser, the refusee has a number of options available, most of which will be interpreted as some kind of response to the refusal (see Figure 1, Chapter One). In a two-person interaction, barring communication breakdown or interruption, this orientation to the refusal usually continues until an outcome is reached or the topic is dropped or changed.[51]

3. Getting the interaction back "on track"

In this chapter, we focus on data from interactions between native speakers and low proficiency non-native speakers. We selected the interactions with the low level speakers as opposed to the higher-level speakers because they provide a better opportunity to focus on the discourse work that the native speaker does.

As discussed earlier, what we suggest is that the native speaker's expectations may affect not only his/her interpretation of the non-native speaker's responses, but may influence the native speaker to attempt to guide the conversation back into the expected mold, that is, to bring the conversation back within expected boundaries.[52] Based on previous research, we assume that both participants in a cross-cultural refusal encounter come to the interaction with their own expectations of how the encounter will proceed. The native speaker is often confronted with the problem of interpreting not only what the non-native speaker means or intends, but also how the non-native speaker's response fits into the native speaker's range of expected moves. Thus, when the native speaker receives a response that does not conform to her notion of what could or should come next, she often finds herself in the uncomfortable position of attempting to reestablish her place in the expected sequence.

In reports on highly proficient non-native speakers of English, researchers such as Gumperz, Jupp, and Roberts (1979) have shown that deviations from expected rhetorical organization or intonation may be treated as the product of rudeness, ignorance, or lack of cooperation. Perhaps because of the low proficiency of the non-native speakers in this study, the native speaker often treats what she sees as inappropriate (e.g., rude, inadequate, confusing) as a problem to be resolved in order to get the conversation back on track, rather than as the result of stupidity or of an intention to derail the interaction. In other words, with low level learners (as opposed to higher proficiency non-native speakers of a language, to whom a native speaker might be quick to attribute rudeness or some personality difficulty or national stereotype), there is often a greater attempt to work out the difficulty that may at first seem to be confusing.

The native speakers in our data use three major approaches for getting the interaction back on track. In situations in which non-native speaker responses either do not correspond to "expected" native speaker behavior in comparable situations (e.g., as described by Beebe, Takahashi, and Uliss-Weltz 1990) or appear unclear or self-contradictory, native speakers react in ways which can be seen as attempts to bring the conversation back to a point within the range of acceptable moves. They do this by 1) requesting reasons for the refusals when they are not provided, 2) indicating unacceptability when their sense of social appropriateness is violated by the content of a non-native speaker's response, or 3) attempting to establish what the non-native speaker will commit to by, for example, repeating established or agreed-upon propositions, especially those related to preconditions on acceptance or refusal. In what follows we present examples of each of these types of responses.

3.1. *Requests for reasons*

The first approach we deal with is requests for reasons. As we noted in previous chapters, Beebe, Takahashi, and Uliss-Weltz (1990) have indicated that it is typical in American English to offer a reason for a refusal in a wide number of situations. Some sort of explanation in such a situation is expected, if not required, in order to avoid a "break in social relations", as Labov and Fanshel (1977) have noted.[53] Thus, it is reasonable to assume that an American English speaker generally expects a reason to accompany a refusal, whereas for Japanese speakers reasons are less often forthcoming. In our data, when a reason is not proffered, the native speaker asks for a reason or at times even provides one. In Example (54), she asks for one.

(54) Haircut situation

    NS: ...um I can I can cut your hair the same way
               I'm very good at this sort of thing I did that
               myself isn't that wonderful? let me see=
                                       [
    NNS: I'm sorry
    NS: =let me get my scissors? ok? all right
    NNS: no thank you huh
→ NS: why not?

In Example (55), the native speaker also does not get the expected explanation, but here, rather than asking a direct question, as in Example (54), she provides a possible reason why the non-native speaker might be declining the invitation.

(55) Skydiving situation

    1   NS: you will go skydiving?
    2   NNS: ah no
    3   NS: no?
    4   NNS: ((nods))
→ 5   NS: no no what ((laughs)) no you don't like to skydive?

In this example, as in Example (54), the native speaker indicates her surprise and/or discomfort at not receiving an explanation by echoing the non-native speaker's negative response in line 3. After the non-native speaker confirms the native speaker's "echo" with a nod (line 4), the native speaker prods for a reason by offering a possible candidate (line 5).

3.2. *Unacceptable moves*

The second approach that we find is one in which native speakers indicate the unacceptability of what in their frame of reference appears to be an inappropriate response. This is illustrated in Example (56).

(56) Haircut situation

        NS: ah how do you like my children's haircuts
        NNS: oh it's very beautiful but like uh- a little ugly (..) o ah
                a little
→   NS: are you serious?
        NNS: uh- sorry
→   NS: you think my children's haircuts are ugly?
        NNS: but it's uh very comfortable I look look I look always
                very comf- comfortable
        NS: very comfortable

The inappropriateness of the non-native speaker's comment (that the children's haircuts are a little ugly) is perhaps more a function of the learner's English proficiency than of transfer of native language semantic content.[54] However, the fact that the native speaker draws attention to the non-native speaker's social blunder indicates her unwillingness (or inability) to continue the interaction until the non-native speaker has been made aware of his *faux pas*.

If it is the case that non-native speakers regularly receive such obvious indications that the content of inappropriate contributions is unacceptable, it is not surprising that researchers such as Bardovi Harlig and Hartford (1993) report that the ability of non-native speakers in ESL situations (e.g., studying at U.S. universities) to choose appropriate semantic formulas and content improves over time without explicit classroom instruction.

3.3. *Establishing propositions "in play"*

Finally, the third approach which the native speakers in our data use is not so much related to situations in which the non-native speaker provides an unacceptable response, but rather situations in which the non-native speaker's response or sequence of responses may leave the native speaker uncertain as to what the non-native speaker is willing to commit to. In these situations, the native speakers in our data attempt to establish what propositions are currently in play before proceeding. In other words, this is an opportunity to get propositions on the table.

Labov and Fanshel (1977) point out that requests can be "renewed if the conditions governing the account can be shown to have changed" (p. 88). Clearly, this presupposes that there are agreed-upon conditions. The native speakers in our data use the interaction itself to establish what those conditions are. They do this by restating or repeating non-native speaker propositions, that is, by 1) restating what they understand as previously established non-native speaker propositions, 2) repeating what they have understood the non-native speaker to have intended or conveyed before responding to it, and 3) restating what they understand the non-native speaker to have agreed to, followed by a brief statement of a consequence or implication.

Examples (57-59) illustrate the native speakers' attempts to establish the propositions in play. In Examples (57) and (58) (taken from role plays with two different non-native speakers), the host mother offers to cut the non-native speaker's hair. She tells the non-native speaker that she has cut her own children's hair and shows her children's haircut for the non-native speaker to admire. In Example (57), the native speaker moves to establish that the non-native speaker indeed likes her children's haircuts, perhaps setting up a basis for her offer.

(57) Haircut situation

> Lines a and b occur early on in the interaction, functioning as a type of pre-offer.

a.	NS:	oh you see my children's haircuts? what do you think of that
b	NNS:	oh good

> [There follows an extended interaction in which the NS offers to cut the NNS's hair and the NNS politely refuses]

	1	NS:	y'di-I c'n I can I cut your hair
	2	NNS:	uh
→	3	NS:	I mean um you like their haircuts right?
	4	NNS:	um
→	5	NS:	you like my my children's haircuts?
	6	NNS:	yes
→	7	NS:	yes?
	8	NNS:	no ((breathy exhalation))
→	9	NS:	eh- you don't like the haircuts[55]

Clearly, the native speaker finds the lack of response in line 2 inadequate and shifts the conversation to the reestablishment of the non-native speaker's position (line 3). Finding the response in line 4 also inadequate, she once again attempts to reestablish the conditions, as can be seen in lines 5 and 7; with the non-native speaker's abrupt shift in line 8 the non-native speaker tries again (in line 9) to articulate a proposition to which the non-native speaker will commit.

A variation on this theme is the native speaker's reformulation or restatement of a non-native speaker's proposition/position before responding to the offer, or a "getting your house in order" response, as in Example (58).

(58) Haircut situation

NS   ...let me get the scissors here
NNS: mm I I um I um I like this um hair like m cool
NS: yes I-I- maybe I could trim a little bit in the back
        there
NNS: nuh? nuh?
                [
NS: uhn yes yes I mean I mean it it would make it
        even cooler if I cut it even more
NNS: more?
NS: yes
NNS: not more
NS: no?
NNS: no
NS: ok um are you sure?
NNS: no sure
→ NS: you're not sure so would you like me to cut your hair?
NNS: a little little bit
NS: a little
                [
NNS: please please
→ NS: a-a-a little? ok where where in the back?

In this example, the native speaker guides the non-native speaker through a series of formulations and reformulations into the determination of relevant propositions or positions, which she restates ("you're not sure"; "a-a-a little?") and then responds to (...so "would you like me to cut your hair?" and "...ok where where in the back?"). Thus, the native speaker is in some sense setting the scene so that she highlights what she is responding to. [56]

Yet another variation is the statement of the consequences of a proposition. That is, not only is a proposition itself made clear, but also consequences of the proposition are laid on the table. In the next example (Example 59) the non-native speaker is eating breakfast and has just been asked if she would be willing to give a speech in church that morning.

(59) Speech at church situation

1	NS	can I help you with your speech?
2	NNS:	nn
3	NS:	um for instance if you want to talk about university life
4	NNS:	mm NOD
5	NS:	can I help you um to use good English? you can ask me what to say
6	NNS:	mm mm mm NOD NOD NOD
7	NS:	we can practice together (..) is that all right?
8	NNS:	yes NOD
→ 9	NS:	oh ok then you can give a speech because you will know what to say
10	NNS:	I don't know HS----------

Here the native speaker offers help, explaining in lines 3-7 what the offer entails. In line 8 the non-native speaker seemingly accepts the native speaker's offer. In line 9 the native speaker spells out the consequences of the non-native speaker's agreement.

Clearly, the native speaker's checks for agreement and statements of consequences did not guarantee comprehension on either side, as the non-native speaker's back channels were not necessarily intended to convey agreement, but nevertheless seem to have been interpreted as doing so. However, what is interesting here is the native speaker's explicit statement of the consequences of the (presumed) agreement.

Thus, native speakers intervene to remedy what they perceive as their partner's demonstrated or potential deficiency, that is, failure to provide 1) essential semantic formulas, 2) appropriate semantic content, and 3) attitudes or responses consistent with or showing commitment to previously conveyed or accepted propositions. They do so by providing missing formulas, questioning or indicating distress at inappropriate semantic content, and restating non-native speaker propositions.

4. Conclusion

There are a number of interesting points about these data. One point to note has to do with the issue of negotiation. As we pointed out in the beginning of this chapter, most of the second language acquisition literature deals with negotiation of meaning at the local level. In fact, some of the data that we have looked at would in that framework be characterized as meaning negotiation by researchers in second language acquisition. For example, in Example (58), the native speaker response in the last line ("a-a-a little?") would be viewed only as a request for confirmation within the input/interaction framework (see Gass 1997 for an elaboration). While this may indeed be a negotiation of meaning sequence in the classic second language acquisition sense, it can also be seen within this broader context of the native speaker's attempting to get the non-native speaker back on track, what one might refer to as "negotiation of discourse."

Perhaps the most significant finding is that the native speaker in these data, because she is the one who made the initial request, is frequently in the position of seeming to guide the conversation onto clearer or more expected and hence familiar ground. That is, within a sequence, such as a refusal sequence, there is a range of possible acceptable conversational paths which can be taken on the road to an outcome. Importantly, these paths may differ from culture to culture, language to language. In cross-cultural interactions participants may find themselves in the position of bringing the conversation back to one of the paths which is acceptable and familiar within their own frame of reference. In other words, speakers may find themselves disoriented and needing to reorient the discourse and their place within that discourse as they move towards an outcome. In this chapter we have seen some of the various means that native speakers of English may use with lower proficiency speakers to bring this about.

With regard to language learning, we suggest that the "reorientations" on the part of the native speaker may serve to make the learner aware of a mismatch, the nature of which she or he may or may not be able to accurately determine. We also suggest that the perception of a mismatch is probably more likely to occur with advanced learners (as for example, the non-native speaker in Example 51) than with less proficient learners. This is so because one undoubtedly needs a firmer linguistic base before being able to recognize the more subtle manipulation of language to meet pragmatic needs.

Chapter 8
Language use and language learning

1. Introduction

In Chapter One we dealt with differences between second language acquisition research and second language use research. The focus so far in this book has been primarily on the communicative behavior of non-native speakers (language use) with particular emphasis on how non-native speakers not only use a limited set of linguistic resources to convey a wide range of organizational and affective cues or messages, but also manage to test, discriminate, and refine many of the linguistic aspects of refusals as they do so. In this chapter we will shift our focus to the native speaker's contributions, looking particularly at native speaker responses to the non-native speaker. We will be speculating that these responses can have an orienting or instructional function in the L2 pragmatic development of non-native speakers. Before making our argument regarding second language pragmatic knowledge, and in order to establish a framework for learning, we will consider, in the first part of this chapter, general issues relating to second language acquisition. The emphasis will be on second language learning as a function of oral interaction. We will briefly touch upon issues that relate to formal models of learning because we see them as applicable beyond the realm of core grammar. In other words, we turn to issues of traditional second language acquisition research. These were briefly touched upon in Chapter Seven in our distinction between global discourse and local linguistic factors and in our discussion in section 4 in this chapter relating to the need for learners to be aware of a mismatch between their own production and the production of speakers of the target language.

2. Second language acquisition, negotiation of meaning, and negative evidence

Early research on second language conversations focused on the language used by native speakers when conversing with non-native speakers. Much of that early literature concentrated on what is known as *foreigner talk* and was concerned with the linguistic modifications which native speakers make when speaking with linguistically deficient non-native speakers, finding, for example such well-documented phenomena as slower speech rate, louder speech, simplified syntax, paucity of slang, and simple vocabulary (see Gass 1997).

Long (1980) noted, however, another important phenomenon which has come to be known in the second language acquisition literature as interactional modification. He found that not only can the actual speech of the native speaker differ when addressing a non-native speaker, but the entire conversational structure may be affected as well. That is, conversations involving non-proficient non-native speakers contain considerably more interactional modifications than do conversations involving only non-native speakers of a language. Such modifications include confirmation checks as in (60), comprehension checks as in (61) and clarification requests as in (62).

(60)   Confirmation check (from Varonis & Gass 1985a)

        NNS1: When can you go to visit me?
        NNS2: visit?

(61)   Comprehension check (from Varonis & Gass 1985a)

        NNS1: and your family have some ingress
        NNS2: yes ah, OK OK
        NNS1: more or less OK?

(62)   Clarification request (from Varonis & Gass 1985a)

        NNS1: ...research
        NNS2: research, I don't know the meaning

Other modification types also exist, for example, reformulations such as "or choice" questions as in Example (63) where the native speaker asks a question and upon an obvious sign of non-comprehension rephrases the question giving alternatives for the non-native speaker to choose from.

(63)   From Varonis and Gass (1985b)

        NS: What did you want? A service call?
        NNS: uh 17 inch huh?
        NS: What did you want a service call? or how much to repair a TV?

Other modifications include decomposed questions as in Examples (64) and (65)

(64)   From Larsen-Freeman and Long (1991)

        NS: When do you go to the uh Santa Monica?
               You say you go fishing in Santa Monica, right?
        NNS: Yeah
        NS: When?

(65)   Eavesdropped by Gass

        NS: Where do you eat your daily meals?
        NNS: Daily meals?
        NS: Lunch and dinner, where do you eat them?

and recasts, as in (66).

(66)   From Philp (1999)

NNS: why he want this house?
NS: why does he want this house?

In Example (64), the native speaker decomposes the original question "When do you go to the uh Santa Monica?" into two parts. First the native speaker establishes the place and the event, that is, fishing in Santa Monica, and then asks the question of the time. Similarly, in Example (65), the native speaker asks a question that is clearly met with non-understanding "daily meals?" The native speaker defines *daily meals* by giving examples *lunch, dinner.* In (66) the native speaker rephrases (recasts) the original incorrect utterance into a correct one. These phenomena have been well-discussed in various articles and books in the second language literature (Gass 1997; Gass and Varonis 1985, Long 1980, 1996; Pica and Doughty 1985; Wesche 1994, among others). What is clear is that interactional modifications in native/non-native talk form an important part of what has come to be known as *negotiation of meaning*, whereby the language of the communicative act is negotiated so that the speakers involved agree (or attempt to agree) on linguistic meanings.

Within this framework the scope of inquiry has been on the form of language employed by interactants and the effect of the interaction itself on the development of second language knowledge.

2.1. *Interaction hypothesis*

Long's (1996) updated version of the Interaction Hypothesis is as follows:

> ...*negotiation for meaning,* and especially negotiation work that triggers *interactional* adjustments by the NS or more competent interlocutor, facilitates acquisition because it connects input, internal learner capacities, particularly selective attention, and output in productive ways (pp. 451-2).

Basic to the interaction hypothesis is the recognition of the importance of conversation as a driving force of second language acquisition. An earlier view of acquisition held that learners learned grammatical rules and then practiced these rules within a conversational setting; classroom drills, classroom interactions, daily interactions with native speakers and so forth were considered only as a means of reinforcing the grammatical rules somehow acquired by a learner. Beginning more than two decades ago with work by Wagner-Gough and Hatch (1975) and developed in the following years by many researchers, (see for example Gass, Mackey and Pica 1998; Gass and Varonis 1985, 1989; Long 1980, 1981, 1983a; Pica 1987, 1988; Pica and Doughty 1985; Pica, Doughty and Young 1986; Pica, Young and Doughty 1987; and Varonis and Gass 1985a), second language research has emphasized the role which negotiated interaction between native and non-native speakers and between two non-native speakers plays in the development of a second language. Within the current orthodoxy, conversation is not only a medium of practice, but it is also the means by which learning takes place. In other words, conversational interaction in a second language forms the basis for the development of syntax rather than being only a forum for practice of grammatical structures.

The interaction hypothesis (Long 1981, 1983a, 1996) builds on the central role of conversation, particularly the notion of negotiation of meaning, suggesting that negotiation facilitates acquisition in that during negotiation, a learner's attention is focused on particular problematic parts of the conversation. An example of what is meant by negotiation within the second language literature is given in Example (67).

(67)   From Pica (1994:514)

   NNS: The windows are crozed
   NS.   The windows have what?
   NNS: closed
   NS: crossed? I'm not sure what you're saying here
   NNS: windows are closed
   NS: oh the windows are closed oh OK sorry

In this example the non-native speaker talks about the windows being *crozed* which the native speaker, quite understandably, had difficulty understanding ("I'm not sure what you're saying here"). Thus, the response "the windows have what?" indicates to the non-native speaker that there is a problem to which the non-native speaker responds with a reformulation *closed*. Once again, the native speaker does not understand and indicates so by saying "crossed?" followed by an overt statement indicating non-understanding. The non-native speaker responds one more time, this time with additional context "windows are closed." The native speaker finally closes the negotiation routine with a reaction to the response, and, in this case, an apology for the interaction "oh the windows are closed oh OK sorry." The example illustrates the local linguistic focus of much standard second language acquisition research.

The following more lengthy example shows how negotiation sequences, in this case exchanges in which the native speaker provides a recast of the learner's incorrect utterance, lead to the learner's recognition of an error and her eventual self-correction.

(68)   From Philp (1999)

> NNS: what ah what the hairstyle is she?
> NS: what hairstyle does she have?
> NNS: what hairstyle does she has?

> [Later turn]

> NNS: what what color is she has=does she has?
> NS: what color is her hair? Ah her hair is blonde
> NNS: is is she makeup?
> NS: mm does she have makeup?
> NNS: does she has makeup?

> [Later turn]

> NNS: what kinds of pet ah does she has?
> NS: she has= what kind of pet does she have?

NNS: what kinds of pet does she have?

In the first sequence the non-native speaker, after the native speaker's rewording of her utterance, corrects the auxiliary from *is* to *does* although the verb form remains incorrect. After a series of negotiation sequences with the native speaker supplying the correct form, the non-native speaker recognizes the verb form error and produces *have* rather than *has*.

What is perhaps most interesting about conversations involving non-native speakers is the complexity of these negotiation routines. In particular, one clarification may often be the trigger for another negotiation sequence.

In sum, negotiation occurs when there is some recognized asymmetry between message transmission and reception and when both participants are willing to attempt a resolution of the difficulty.

The attention to problematic language areas is a first step in learning. As Gass and Varonis (1994) argued

> [negotiations] crucially focus the learner's attention on the parts of the discourse that are problematic, either from a productive or a receptive point of view. Attention in turn is what allows learners to notice a gap between what they produce/know and what is produced by speakers of the L2. The perception of a gap or mismatch may lead to grammar restructuring (p. 299).

Long (1996) similarly notes that

> These qualities of negotiation work, in other words, may function to focus the learner on form in a similar way that input enhancement appears to do in the classroom.....Heightened attention makes detection both of new forms and of mismatches between input and output more likely, and such mismatches may also provide at least some of the information a learner needs about what is *not* permissible in a language (p. 453).

In the following section we introduce the concept of negative evidence, a central concept in the second language acquisition literature and also central to the theoretical arguments surrounding the interaction hypothesis. This discussion is followed by a general discussion on different types of evidence that are available to learners as they attempt to construct a system of linguistic knowledge of the second language.

2.2. *Language knowledge*

The main questions asked by language acquisition researchers (both first and second) are the following: How are languages learned? How do learners come up with a rich knowledge of language which, at least in the case of children, takes place in a short period of time. This knowledge, for both children learning a first language and adults learning a second language, includes sentence level knowledge of grammaticality. In other words, knowing a language means *inter alia* having a grammatical system that allows learners to discern which sentences are grammatical and which are ungrammatical. The question of concern to first and second language researchers is: How does this knowledge come about given that exposure to language is insufficiently rich to enable one to formulate a complex grammatical system? What evidence is necessary to allow complex linguistic knowledge to come about?

Throughout the recent literature, two more or less distinct positions regarding the necessary evidence requirements for learning can be discerned. In general terms, we can summarize these as the nature versus nurture positions.[57] The first refers to the possibility that learners (whether child first language learners or adult second language learners) come to the learning situation with innate knowledge about language; the second position claims that language development is inspired and conditioned by the environment, that is, the interactions in which learners engage.

Much of the debate centers around certain kinds of knowledge and how learners (children/adults) can possibly attain that knowledge without being explicitly taught it or without being exposed to it in some direct way. For purposes of exposition, we make the assumption that part of our knowledge of language consists of abstract principles.

The main research question concerns the possibility of learning a complex set of abstractions when the input alone does not contain evidence of these abstractions. If the input does not provide the information necessary for the extraction of abstractions, there must be something in addition to the input that children use in grammar formation. Universal Grammar is hypothesized to be an innate language faculty that limits the kinds of languages that can be created (for references in the second language acquisition literature, see Cook 1988, 1993; L. White 1989). It thus serves as a constraint on the kinds of grammars that can be created and in a sense limits the hypothesis space that learners (children and possibly adults learning a second language) use in creating linguistic knowledge.

We turn to an examination of the kinds of complexities and abstractions that appear not to be available from the input, thereby considering what it means to say that the input is insufficient. Consider the following examples from English, all based on the possibility of contracting *want to* to *wanna*:

(69)	The students want to go to Niagara Falls.
(70)	The students wanna go to Niagara Falls.
(71)	Visa, it's everywhere you want to be. (American TV slogan)
(72)	Visa, it's everywhere you wanna be.
(73)	Ethan wants to go, but Seth and Aaron don't want to.
(74)	Ethan wants to go, but Seth and Aaron don't wanna.
(75)	Do Tianwei and Pat want to go to the party tonight?
(76)	Do Bob and Ursula wanna go to the party tonight?
(77)	Who do Josh and Sue want to see?
(78)	Who do Aaron, Seth, and Ethan wanna see?
(79)	Who do you want to spread the rumor about?
(80)	Who do you wanna spread the rumor about?

While all of the above sentences are possible in English, there are numerous instances in which no contraction of *want to* to *wanna* is possible. Consider the following:

(81)	Who do India and John want to spread the rumor?
(82)	*Who do India and John wanna spread the rumor?

or consider the following pair of sentences, the first of which is ambiguous ("I want to succeed Josh" and "I want Josh to succeed") whereas the second is not (only the first reading is possible):

(83)   Josh is the man I want to succeed.
(84)   Josh is the man I wanna succeed.

Because there is nothing in the input that will inform a learner of the possibilities and impossibilities of contraction, something else must provide that information since clearly this information is part of what adult speakers know about English. It is at this point that Universal Grammar is invoked and specifically the concept of traces, part of a Universal Grammar principle[58] needed to account for a range of syntactic phenomena.[59] In other words, the standard explanation to account for this phenomenon of acquisition is that these constraints are not learned *per sé* (and cannot be learned given that the relevant information is not available through the input). Rather, the knowledge which allows us to understand this linguistic information is a reflection of the biological predisposition that humans have toward the organization of language.

While there is still considerable disagreement as to the nature of Universal Grammar, there is wide-spread agreement among linguists that there is some sort of innately specified knowledge that children are born with. The arguments assume that acquisition is dynamic and must take into account not only details of linguistic knowledge and how that knowledge comes to be, but also how language develops as a function of interactions in which learners engage. The question then is how innate knowledge interacts with the environment/input in the creation of linguistic knowledge.

The question could be raised, as indeed it was during the days in which behaviorist theories of language acquisition were in vogue, concerning correction. Why does one need to posit an innate language faculty when it could be claimed that correction is a vital part of language acquisition? In other words, when errors occur, they are just 'corrected' right out of the system. However, this is not an adequate explanation for at least two reasons: 1) Children do not receive large doses of correction and 2) When so-called correction takes place, it is often not perceived as such.

2.3. *Specific kinds of evidence*

From the perspective of learning, the question is: "How do we come to have such rich and specific knowledge, or such intricate systems of belief and understanding, when the evidence available to us is so meager?" (Chomsky 1987, cited in Cook 1988: 55). From a theoretical perspective there are at least three kinds of evidence that learners can avail themselves of in the process of learning: positive evidence, negative evidence, and indirect negative evidence.

2.3.1. Positive evidence

Positive evidence refers to the input and for the sake of simplicity is basically comprised of the set of well-formed sentences to which learners are exposed. These utterances are available from either the spoken language (or visual language in the case of sign language) and/or from the written language. This is the most direct means that learners have available to them from which they can form linguistic hypotheses. As discussed above, positive evidence is insufficient for the development of a complete grammar (see L. White 1989). Similarly, Bardovi-Harlig and Hartford (1996) in research on interlanguage pragmatics with a focus on advising sessions, discuss positive evidence as it relates to the development of interlanguage pragmatics in institutional settings.

2.3.2. Negative evidence

Negative evidence refers to the type of information that is provided to learners concerning the incorrectness of an utterance. This might be in the form of explicit or implicit information. The following are examples of explicit negative evidence and implicit negative evidence respectively.

(85)   I seed the man.
        No, we say "I saw the man"

(86)   I seed the man
        What?

In Example (85), the child learner is receiving direct information about the ungrammaticality of what was said, whereas in the second example, ungrammaticality must be inferred. In Example (86) it is, of course, possible that the learner will not understand that this is intended as a correction and may only think that the speaker really did not hear what was said. As a summary of the two evidence types discussed thus far, Long (in press) provides a useful taxonomy, reproduced in Figure 11.

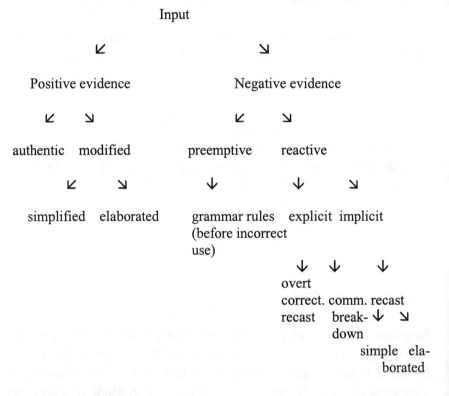

Figure 11. Evidence types

Evidence can be positive or negative. If positive, it can be either authentic or modified. If modified, it can be simplified or elaborated. Negative evidence can also be of two types: preemptive (occurring before an actual error — as in a classroom context) or reactive. If reactive, it can be explicit or implicit. Explicit evidence is an overt correction. Implicit evidence can result in a communication breakdown or in a recast. Recasts, in turn, can be simple (a repetition) or elaborated (a change to a [generally] grammatical form). Within the context of second language learning, negative evidence can be thought of as feedback. A common position maintains that a theory of how children learn language cannot rely on negative evidence in as much as it is inconsistent both in its provision and in its effect; it is not clear the extent to which this position is viable in the case of second language acquisition. We return to this discussion below.

2.3.3. Indirect negative evidence

Indirect negative evidence is perhaps the most interesting of the types of evidence available to learners, but unfortunately is the least studied, perhaps because no theoretical argument rests crucially on it. Plough (1994: 30) defines indirect negative evidence as an "indirect means of letting the learner know that a feature is not possible because it is never present in the *expected* environment." She further points out that the term "indirect negative evidence" is a misnomer since it is not a form of indirect correction, or any sort of correction.

It may be easier to understand this concept in second language acquisition than in first since a crucial part of the notion rests on the concept of *expected environment*. Where would those expectations come from? Essentially, there are two choices: from the innately specified principles and parameters of Universal Grammar or from the first language (or other languages known). Imagine an English speaker learning Italian. This individual hears sentences without subjects as in Example (87):

(87) *Vado   al   cinema stasera.*
      go (1 sg.) to the   movies this evening
      'I'm going to the movies this evening.'

(88)   *Mangiamo   a casa domani.*
      eat (1st pl.) at home tomorrow
      'We're eating at home tomorrow.'

(89)   *Va   a Parigi sabato.*
      go (3 sg.) to Paris Saturday
      'He's going to Paris on Saturday.'

Because there is a domain of expectations of obligatory subjects based on this learner's knowledge of English, this learner is likely to notice the absence of them in Italian.

Given the possibility that negative evidence cannot be relied on in language acquisition (particularly child language acquisition), some other learning mechanism must be invoked. Lasnik (1989) and others (e.g., Archibald 1993; Saleemi 1992; Valian 1990) have argued that indirect negative evidence may be able to fill in for the fact that direct negative evidence is not reliably and consistently present. (See Plough 1994 for an in-depth review of this research.)

2.4. *Availability of evidence*

Earlier views of language acquisition were based on a behaviorist view of language. Central to this view was the role of correction. Children were imagined to learn language through a process of imitation and analogizing (cf. Bloomfield 1933 and Gass and Selinker 1994 for a synthesis). It was well accepted that imitation was often faulty and there needed to be some theoretical mechanism to correct faulty forms. That mechanism was correction — either in the form of direct correction, such as informing a child that a form used was incorrect, or in the form of non-comprehension ("I don't understand you") or not providing a desired object (a child asks for a toy and doesn't receive it) or a desired outcome (a child wants to go outside and the adult does not respond appropriately).

Earlier, we briefly discussed the concept of negative evidence, as it applies to child language acquisition. Negative evidence is a crucial concept since it forms the basis of the innateness argument: The need for innateness stems from the lack of consistent correction.

Central to this argument is the fact that direct intervention in which incorrect utterances are corrected is not consistently present in the learning environment. And, further, when such correction is available, it may be sufficient to inform a child that a particular utterance is incorrect, but it often does not tell the child what needs to be done to correct the utterance and hence to revise a current hypothesis. The examples below illustrate that even when children do receive correction and even when they are informed about the appropriate modification, their grammars are often impervious to suggestions about change.

(90)   From Cazden (1972: 92); no age given
   Child: My teacher holded the baby rabbits and we patted them.
   Adult: Did you say your teacher held the baby rabbits?
   Child: Yes.
   Adult: What did you say she did?
   Child: She holded the baby rabbits and we patted them.
   Adult: Did you say she held them tightly?
   Child: No, she holded them loosely.

(91)   From McNeill (1966: 69); no age given
   Child: Nobody don't like me.
   Mother: No, say "nobody likes me."
   Child: Nobody don't like me.

   [Eight repetitions of this dialogue]

   Mother: No, now listen carefully; say "nobody likes me."
   Child: Oh! Nobody don't likes me.

(92)   Child, Age = 3, Gass, as participant
   Child: I don't see no trees.
   Mother: I don't see any trees. Not no trees, any trees.

Child: No any trees. No any trees.
Mother: I don't see any trees.

In each of these examples, there is some attempt to provide feedback to the child concerning the incorrectness of an hypothesis. In the first example, the attempt is made through correct modeling of the irregular past tense; yet the child continued to use the regular past tense form. In the second and third examples, there is an attempt by the mother to model and even to overtly instruct the child as to the correct form. In both instances, these attempts fail and the child continues to use the original form.

Given the absence of useable and/or used negative evidence, some additional means must be made available to a learner in order to eventually learn the type of abstractions discussed earlier and to disallow overgeneralized grammars from which one cannot "retreat" on the basis of positive evidence alone. Universal Grammar is what has been posited to satisfy these conditions. In other words, because there is no way through positive evidence alone to limit the range of possible sentences and since negative evidence is not frequently and consistently forthcoming, there must be innate principles which constrain *a priori* the possibilities of grammar formation.

For second language learning similar arguments have been made, that is, because of a lack of negative evidence, one needs to assume that adults have access to the same innate universal constraints as children (see arguments in Schwartz 1993). However, there is a crucial difference: It is not clear that the assumption of lack of negative evidence in second language acquisition is warranted (Birdsong 1989; Gass 1988; Schachter 1988). If we consider that negative evidence is present primarily in conversational interactions, then it becomes necessary to investigate the nature and structure of conversations to understand the potential role of negative evidence in the acquisition of a second language.

3. Attention and noticing

The concept of attention and the related notion of "noticing" figure crucially in this debate, as these concepts are basic to the interaction hypothesis and to the value of negative evidence for learning. It is what allows learners to notice what needs to be learned.

Much recent second language acquisition literature has focused on the concept of attention. Given that second language learners are surrounded by second language data, some mechanism must be available to help them wade through and sort out these data. One way in which the input becomes more manageable is by focusing attention on a limited and hence controlled amount of data at a given point in time. By limiting the data to which one attends, learners can create a data set that allows them to formulate a second language system; they are able through attentional devices to "tune in" some stimuli and to "tune out" others. James' (1907) very early definition characterizes attention as "...the taking possession by the mind, in clear and vivid form, of one out of what seems several simultaneously possible objects or trains of thought" (cited in Posner 1994).

Another concept that is frequently discussed in the literature is awareness. Definitions are somewhat scattered, but a common one according to Schachter, Rounds, Wright, and Smith (in press) is that "an individual is able to detect and verbalize the pattern that he has learned" (p. 2).

One of the early works devoted to the role of attention in SLA was that of Schmidt (1990, 1992, 1993b, 1994). Schmidt's main point is that noticing something in the input is crucial to its subsequent role in acquisition. That is, before something can serve as intake, it must be noticed. Gass (1997) uses the term *apperception* which serves as a priming device for learning. In other words, learners must *apperceive* input before they can use that input for learning. Where Gass (1997) and Schmidt part company is that for Schmidt "intake is that part of the input that the learner notices" (Schmidt 1990: 139). Thus, for Schmidt once the learner notices something in the input, it automatically becomes intake: "If noticed, it becomes intake" (Schmidt 1990: 139). Gass (1997: 101) argues that

> The input-interaction view must take the position that noticing is crucial. In negotiation the learner is focusing on linguistic form, and that focus, or specific attention paid to linguistic form, is the first step toward grammar change.

Schmidt (1993a, 1993b) argues that noticing involves a subjective experience and an ability to articulate that experience. While Schmidt (1993a: 25) acknowledges that determining what a learner has or has not noticed is virtually impossible, at least in naturalistic learning situations, he does claim that one can show that something has not been noticed "by the failure of subjects to report their awareness of a stimulus if asked immediately following its presentation."[60]

A major impetus for Schmidt's view of noticing as involving consciousness and awareness as necessary conditions for acquisition comes from his own diary studies when he was in Brazil learning Portuguese. During a five-month stay in Brazil he studied Portuguese formally (5 weeks), spent time interacting with native speakers of Portuguese, and kept diary records. Additionally, he arranged to be tape-recorded at one month intervals. In trying to determine the relationship between noticing and eventual output, his notes (diary, class notes) were compared with the tape recordings of his speech. These records were analyzed in a number of ways. For example, there was an attempt to see if the relationship between frequency in the input and eventual output could be established. While there was some relationship, it was insufficient to account for what Schmidt actually produced. What did appear to be significant was the relationship between what he noted in his diary (either by forms that he wrote down or by notes that he wrote about the forms) and the emergence of these forms in his speech. As Schmidt (1990: 140) notes, he was able to

> identify the apparent source of innovation as something very specific that someone had said to me that had caught my attention, such as the following example:
>
> *Journal entry, Week 21*...I'm suddenly hearing things I never heard before, including things mentioned in class. Way back in the beginning, when we learned questions words, we were told that there are alternate short and long forms like *o que* and *o que é que, quem* or *quem é que.* I have never heard the long forms, ever, and concluded that they were just another classroom fiction. But today, just before we left Cabo Frio, M said something to me that I didn't catch right away. It sounded like French que'est-ce que c'est, only much abbre-

viated, approximately [kekse], which must be *(o) que (e) que (vo)cê...*

Journal entry, Week 22. I just said to N *o que 'e que você quer* but quickly: [kekseker]. Previously, I would have said just *o que*. N didn't blink, so I guess I got it right...

Schmidt goes on to report that these forms had been present in the input. In fact, 43% of the question words on the first tape were of this type. He had "heard them and processed them for meaning from the beginning, but did not notice the form for five months" (1990: 141). It was the overt noticing of the form that Schmidt claims led to his use of the form. Here again Schmidt equates noticing with conscious awareness and ability to articulate since if the forms were processed for meaning, they were "noticed" or apperceived earlier.

Some evidence from second language acquisition that suggests learning without attention or awareness is presented in Gass (1997). These arguments go against the strong version of the noticing hypothesis (Schmidt 1990, 1993a and b):

> Attention to input is a necessary condition for any learning at all, and ... what must be attended to is not input in general, but whatever features of the input play a role in the system to be learned. (Schmidt 1993a:35)

However, the data described in Gass (1997) concerning the acquisition of relative clauses suggests learning with no input and if no input existed, how could attention to input be a necessary condition for all aspects of learning?

Recent experimental work by Schachter, Rounds, Wright, and Smith (in press) suggests that awareness in and of itself (in their work awareness is operationalized by the presentation of explicit rules to learners) is not a determining factor in learning. Another part of their work considered the role of attention. Learners were placed into groups that differed in the extent to which they were required to attend to a particular syntactic feature. While there was evidence of attentional learning, there was also evidence of learning in a non-attentional mode, which indicates that Schmidt's strong hypothesis cannot be maintained.

The preceding arguments are not intended to mean that attention and awareness are not important in the process of learning a second language. The arguments were merely intended to show that they are not the only factors. As is clear, some of the factors involved in second language learning are internal to the learner and others are external to the learner. Those that are internal to the learner are of two sorts, those that are available to introspection and those that are not. Examples of introspective types of internal factors are just those aspects of learning that a learner *can* be aware of, such as, vocabulary, certain grammatical features, etc. These can be manipulated (oriented) by others (e.g., teachers) so as to have a greater likelihood of having attention drawn to them and hence of being noticed. Others are not (readily) available for introspection, and cannot be manipulated. These aspects of language do not require attention or awareness for learning. Examples of the latter may stem from language based on Universal Grammar, or for purposes of this book, pragmatics and speech acts.

The complexity of what is noticed can be illustrated by the following examples taken from Philp (1999), who was concerned with the role of noticing in the acquisition of English question forms.

(93)   From Philp (1999: 170-171)

(a)   NNS: what does she talk
        NS: what is she saying
        NNS: what does she say?

(b)   NNS: she is ah (.) why her mother ah carry on her?
        NS: why is her mother holding her hand?=
        NNS: =holding her hand?=why her mother holding
               her hand?

(c)   NNS: she is happy or- does she happy or sad?
        NS: is she happy or sad?
        NNS: is she happy or sad?

(d)   NNS: what what does she doing?
              NS: what's she doing?
              NNS: What's doing?

              [Later turn]

              NNS: who who is he who does he expecting now?
              NS: who's he expecting?
              NS: =ya=who's expecting?

In example (a) the learner appeared to notice only the difference in the lexical item, but kept the verb form as in the original utterance. In the second example (b), the learner noticed the new lexcial item (*hold* rather than *carry*), but did not incorporate the correction of the auxiliary. However, in example (c), she did notice the auxiliary change, but in example (d), she appeared to notice the auxiliary problem, but failed to notice the pronoun problem. Similarly, a recent study by Mackey and Gass (1998) showed that often what was intended as feedback of one type was not always received as the same type of feedback. For example, feedback on morphosyntax was not always received as morphosyntactic feedback, but may have been interpreted as pronunciation feedback. Hence, what learners take from feedback is variable and may differ from what an interlocutor intends. At times certain features are noticed; at other times, other features are noticed. Proposed functions of negative evidence/correction are illustrated in Figure 12.

Figure 12 shows the function (and types) of negative evidence that are available to second language learners. There are two primary ways in which negative evidence becomes available to learners: negotiation (as seen in the earlier parts of this chapter) and correction (as in "No, that's wrong, you should say it like X"). Both of these negative evidence types have the function of providing the learner with an opportunity to notice that there is some sort of error. The error could be in any area of language (e.g., lexicon, syntax), or with specific reference to the material of this book, pragmatics. Once a learner is aware of an incongruity between what she or he has said and what is appropriate usage in the target language, she or he has to "search the input" for more information. Here there are two possible outcomes, either the input is available or it is not. If it is available, learners can either confirm an hypothesis that they might have generated or will receive disconfirmatory evidence. To take a pragmatic example, let's assume a second language learner who walks into her supervisor's office and says "Give me that book." This directness in English is, of course, inappropriate in most circumstances.[61] Let's further say that the supervisor makes it known that this is inappropriate (perhaps by making a sarcastic remark). This constitutes some form of correction. Let's also assume that the learner notices the error, but isn't certain what the problem is. She or he might then "search" the input for further examples of requests in order to determine what the appropriate way of requesting is.

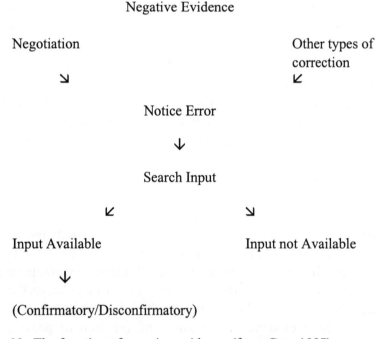

Figure 12. The function of negative evidence (from Gass 1997)

To take a non-hypothetical example, consider the following from Blum-Kulka and Olshtain (1986).

A teacher working with recorded material left a note for the video technician asking him to prepare a copy of a tape for her. The note contained the following: "If it is not too much bother, could you please make a video cassette of this lesson." The technician did what he was supposed to do but added a note of his own: "When have I ever refused to prepare a cassette for you? I'm really surprised at you." (p. 168)

The technician was a native speaker of Hebrew, the teacher was a native speaker of Norwegian (non-native speaker of Hebrew) and the interaction was in Hebrew. To apply our concept of negative evidence, the message left by the technician was an indication of inappropriate behavior, or at the least an indication that something was amiss (the technician interpreted the overly elaborate message as some sort of criticism of his work). As Blum-Kulka and Olshtain note, "The miscommunication that occurred was probably due to a clash in cultural norms relating to manner, realized in this case by the amount of redressive action ... deemed appropriate for the specific request" (p. 168).

Finally, to take a specific example from this book, we repeat Example (56) from Chapter Seven, repeated here as (94).

(94)   Haircut situation

	NS:	ah how do you like my children's haircuts
	NNS:	oh it's very beautiful but like uh- a little ugly (..) o ah a little
→	NS:	are you serious?
	NNS:	uh- sorry
→	NS:	you think my children's haircuts are ugly?
	NNS:	but it's uh very comfortable I look look I look always very comf- comfortable
	NS:	very comfortable

Here, the native speaker is unambiguous in her belief that the non-native speaker's comment concerning the ugliness of the haircuts is inappropriate. As we noted in Chapter Seven, Bardovi-Harlig and Hartford (1993) found from their data that the presence of fairly explicit negative evidence makes it likely that these inappropriate linguistic behaviors will be noticed as such and hence will diminish over time.

4. Interlanguage pragmatics

We have spent considerable time laying the groundwork for a view of how second languages are learned, a view that takes as important the role of face-to-face interaction in providing learners with appropriate information for grammar formation. We have done this within a current orthodox position of second language acquisition research. The learning of pragmatics shares some important characteristics with the learning of core areas of language, and it is these characteristics that we focus on in the remainder of this chapter.

4.1. *The development of pragmatic knowledge*

We now turn to issues that go beyond the realm of core areas of language and turn to the major area of this book — the area of language use in context and the learning of pragmatic information. Literature in the area of interlanguage pragmatics has been concerned not so much with language form but with language use. It differs from the literature on negotiation of meaning in the traditional second language acquisition sense in that it incorporates a broader range of sociolinguistic phenomena, including speech acts.

Bardovi-Harlig (1998) makes the point that there is little in the interlanguage pragmatics literature that is acquisitional in nature. Similarly, Kasper (1992) notes that "the majority of [interlanguage pragmatics] studies focus on use, without much attempt to say or even imply anything about development" (p. 204). Kasper traces the (short) history of interlanguage pragmatics, including its research questions and research methods, to cross-cultural research which, clearly, is not concerned with acquisition at all. Bardovi-Harlig supports the view of the non-acquisitional nature of most interlanguage pragmatics studies with the observation that in most of these studies learners are referred to as *non-native speakers* rather than *learners*.[62] Kasper and Schmidt (1996) (elaborated by Bardovi-Harlig 1998) outline some of the research questions that are of concern to research in interlanguage pragmatics, at least that part of interlanguage pragmatics that focuses on learning as opposed to use. These questions are strikingly similar to those that are asked about second language learning of all areas of language. And, in fact, there is little reason to assume that many of the answers, or at least approaches to questions, are not similar as well. That is, learners need appropriate evidence to determine how to perform speech acts and how to be pragmatically appropriate in a second language. We argue that the same kinds of evidence discussed earlier in this chapter will be germane in the study of pragmatics. Where the acquisition of pragmatics and the acquisition of formal syntax, for example, part company relates to the question of innateness and the principles of Universal Grammar that have been argued to drive the acquisition of syntax. This notion is supported by Kasper and Schmidt (1996: 164) who argue that

> Presumably, most of the same mechanisms as those identified for the acquisition of other cognitive skills will also propel pragmatic development, although not all learning mechanisms discussed in the field of SLA are likely to be implicated; specifically the innate learning mechanisms associated with Universal Grammar theory should play no role because that model of language explicitly excludes considerations of pragmatics or communicative competence (Chomsky, 1980).

Schmidt (1993a) drawing on general theories in human learning (particularly those relating to consciousness) argues that pragmatic knowledge is partly conscious and partly unconscious. This goes contra Wolfson (1989) who argued that rules of speaking (which from her perspective include both pragmatics and discourse)

> ...more generally, norms of interaction are...largely unconscious. What this means is that native speakers, although perfectly competent in the patterns of speech behavior which prevail in their own communities are, with the exception of a few explicitly taught formulas, not even aware of the patterned nature of their speech be-

havior. [Native speakers]...are not able...to describe their own rules of speaking (p. 37).

We assume that Schmidt is correct that some pragmatic forms and some speech act behavior is accessible to awareness and that learners can notice these behaviors. We claim that there is little reason to assume that the principles that we have discussed in previous sections regarding negative evidence and particularly attention and noticing apply to only part of language (syntax or vocabulary), but not other parts of language (e.g., pragmatics). In other words, we argue for a unitary view of language that relies heavily (although perhaps not exclusively) on learners noticing facts of language and using what has been noticed as a springboard for learning. Noticing can, of course, come from one's internal resources or from explicit instruction, for example, through feedback (e.g., error correction, as in Nobuyoshi and Ellis 1993) or explicit rules. Gass (1988) discusses various factors that can lead to learners noticing parts of language and not noticing others including such factors as prior knowledge. In fact, Bardovi-Harlig and Hartford (1996) in their study of the input available in advising sessions argue that one reason for the lack of acquisition of appropriate pragmatic forms in this context is the lack of positive evidence. That is, the encounter that these non-native speakers are in, that of status-unequals in student professor advising, provide no positive evidence from peers as to the appropriate forms in this institutional context.

Schmidt (1993a) presents several examples from his own diary study (Schmidt and Frota 1986) on how learning of pragmatics might take place. His description is similar to descriptions for the learning of language form.

> I noted in my diary several times the difficulties I had with telephone converstions, especially in knowing when and how to end a conversation (Schmidt and Frota 1986, 276). I knew that with friends the closing move would be for both parties to say *ciao*, but I could never identify the point at which I could say it, so I would often stand holding the phone waiting patiently for the other person to say it first. Finally, during the last week of my stay, a friend came to my apartment and used my telephone to make several calls. I listened carefully, and noticed that in two successive calls, shortly

before saying *ciao,* my friend said the phrase *então tá,* which means no more than "so, then." Suspecting that this might be a preclosing formula, I immediately called another friend and after a few minutes of talk, said *então tá,* paused briefly and plunged ahead with *ciao* in the same turn. It worked, and after that I had no trouble at all getting off the phone efficiently. I subsequently asked several native speakers how to close a telephone conversation. None could tell me, but when I suggested the use of *então tá,* they agreed that was right. (p. 29)

This example suggests that just as one can "notice" linguistic form, one can also notice other parts of language, as in this case, how to close a telephone conversation.

It is well established that pragmatic information or speech act behavior represents areas of language that are late learned. That is, even with advanced learners, the ability to use pragmatically appropriate behavior is often lacking (Tannen 1985; Thomas 1983). Blum-Kulka and Olshtain (1986) in their discussion of pragmatic failure in the context of amount of speech, note that non-native speakers use more words than native speakers do in performing similar pragmatic acts. A typical example can be seen in Examples (95) and (96).

(95)   Hebrew speaker in English

I went over the material we will study in the next weeks and I rather like to have your lecture next week, if it's possible and if you can be ready.

(96)   Native speaker of American English

Look, your presentation would be perfect for next week's session. Do you think you could have it ready?

Blum-Kulka and Olshtain make the important point that

What is most significant is the fact that when such pragmatic failure occurs between native speakers of the same language, there is a good chance that the speaker will recognize the failure and the reason for it, and will therefore perform suitable repair. The non-native speaker, however, might be completely unaware of the reason for the failure and may therefore be unable to repair the interaction. (p. 177)

Returning to our concept of negative evidence, there is no easy or obvious way to inform non-native speakers of the inappropriateness of being overly elaborate; hence, there is little way that they will ever be able to remedy the situation. This assumes, of course, that remedy requires an awareness of a problem.

One reason for the difficulty in obtaining appropriate knowledge of the pragmatics of a second language may be an assumption that humans make about learning a second language, namely, that what needs to be learned is the phonology, lexicon and syntax of a second language. Pragmatics and/or speech acts, such as how to request something or how to refuse something, are initially perceived to be universal. Hence, learners are not aware that there is anything to learn. If they are not aware of the learning necessity, they are unlikely to notice subtle differences between languages. And, as we argued above, noting mismatches between target language and native languages is a major driving force in learning.

4.2. *Negotiation of meaning*

In this section we extend the concept of negotiation prevalent in the second language acquisition literature to include not only negotiation of meaning (i.e., negotiation of linguistic form and semantic content), but also what we refer to as negotiation of expectation (see Chapter Seven). In the previous chapter and earlier in this chapter, we presented the following example.

(97) Haircut situation

> NS: ah how do you like my children's haircuts
> NNS: oh it's very beautiful but like uh- a little ugly (..) o ah
>   a little
> →   NS: are you serious?

      NNS: uh- sorry
→   NS: you think my children's haircuts are ugly?
      NNS: but it's uh very comfortable I look look I look always
               very comf- comfortable
      NS: very comfortable

We argue that just as negative evidence is an important part of the learning of syntax, morphosyntax, lexicon, and phonology, it can also be useful as a way of informing learners what is pragmatically inappropriate ("are you serious?" and "you think my children's haircuts are ugly?"). The crucial ingredient is that learners notice what is correct and incorrect, whether it be grammar or language use. Being aware of an incorrect form or an incorrect usage is an initial step in language development.

5. Conclusion

This chapter has been concerned with the relationship of language learning and language use. It has taken as a base the input and inter- action framework in second language acquisition in which language interaction is an important ingredient in the learning process. We have accounted for this framework by considering the evidence re- quirement for learning and the roles of attention and awareness.

We argued that the learning of pragmatics is not fundamentally different from the learning of other parts of language in terms of the mechanisms necessary. This claim must be tempered for certain parts of language for which generalizations cannot be deduced from the available evidence. For pragmatics, there does not appear to be abstract information to be learned and, hence, an innate acquisition device is not necessary.

As with any part of language, we pointed out the need for posi- tive evidence; when positive evidence was not available, as in the Bardovi-Harlig and Hartford (1996) study, there was little evidence of learning. Negative evidence through negotiation (as in Example 96) was also seen to be prevalent in making learners aware of inap- propriateness. That the learner in Example (96) apparently noticed his gaffe is seen by his apology "sorry" and his backtracking in his subsequent turn, when he says "but it's uh very comfortable I look look I look always very comf- comfortable."

We have also dealt with the important concepts of attention and awareness in the learning of all parts of a second language, including second language pragmatics. Bardovi-Harlig and Dörnyei's (1998) study comparing learners of English in a second language environment with learners of English in a foreign language environment showed that those learners in an English as a second language environment are more sensitive to pragmatic infelicities than are those in a foreign language environment (the opposite was found for awareness of grammatical infelicities). What this suggests is that significant input is necessary for learners to recognize pragmatic appropriateness. As we discussed earlier, most learners are not aware at the outset that there is much to be learned in terms of pragmatics. Negative evidence, as in Example (97), may be necessary.

In sum, the learning of pragmatics involves the same kind of informational requirements as does the learning of other parts of language. In this chapter we have attempted to make this link explicit.

Chapter 9
Epilogue

This book has treated a variety of topics through the backdrop of one face-threatening speech act, that of refusals. We have provided a detailed description of the linguistic devices that the non-native speakers in our study used to negotiate their way through a refusal. In so doing, we have dealt with the strategies used, the problem areas revealed, and the interactional resources drawn on when the linguistic knowledge and/or ability needed by the non-native speakers to negotiate their way through a face-threatening encounter were unavailable.

The richness of the data-base that we have presented confirms previous findings that one common and traditional means of gathering data (the discourse completion test) cannot adequately reflect the resources that non-native speakers draw on in refusal encounters. Refusals that are produced spontaneously or, in the case of the data presented in this book, elicited through role plays reveal the ways in which non-native speakers maneuver their way through an uncomfortable sequence.

During these interactions, non-native speakers displayed a sensitivity to pragmatic communication strategies that aided them in bringing about an effective refusal or a harmonious relationship. We identified five strategies that the non-native speakers in our database relied on as they sought to achieve their goals even when they lacked pragmatic abilities in the second language: 1) bluntness (or directness), 2) indications of linguistic or sociocultural inadequacy, 3) use of the first language, 4) sequential shifts (in attention to goal, choice of semantic formula, and choice of content of excuses or alternatives), and 5) nonverbal expressions of affect. Even though these communication strategies were not always successful in achieving an effective refusal and a positive relationship, most attempts proved instrumental in bringing about one or the other.

Through the analyses presented in this book, we have seen the importance of back channels, and, in particular, the difficulty that some non-native speakers may have in coordinating their verbal and non-verbal messages, occasionally leaving a listener puzzled by the resulting response. In considering data from low proficiency non-native speakers and data from more proficient speakers, we noted differences in their coordination of the verbal and the non-verbal. This may suggest a learning trajectory with beginning learners unable to coordinate, due to processing constraints, two separate parts of the linguistic message. Back channels were seen to have strategic functions, being used sparingly when there was a likelihood that any positive response could be taken as an acceptance and being used to show support and empathy when the situation became particularly difficult.

In addition to minimal vocalizations, we have also demonstrated the powerful role that nonverbal information can play in face-threatening speech acts. In particular, we have seen that even though semantic formulas may remain relatively constant across individuals, their nonverbal signals can convey additional information regarding their affective stance with respect to the interlocutor and/or the linguistic message.

An important part of refusal encounters relates to the concept of negotiation, which we have treated in two different ways: negotiation of expectations and negotiation of meaning, including linguistic form, linguistic meaning, and pragmatic appropriateness. With regard to negotiation of expectations, each speaker has his/her own notion of how a refusal sequence should develop. When an expected path is not followed, speakers tend to try to find their footing in the conversation and guide the "wayward" partner onto familiar ground. In our data, the one to take charge was generally the native speaker, perhaps because she was the one who made the initial request and was thus the one to first become disoriented when expectations were not met.

Finally, we have tied the concept of negotiation of expectations to the concept of negotiation of form/meaning used within the second language literature. We have sketched out a view of language learning that places attention at the core. We have further argued that negotiation and other forms of negative evidence are a means of orienting learners to areas of language form and/or use which are incongruous with those of the target language. Negotiation of expectation is a means of reorienting the discourse path and, as such, may serve to alert learners to the fact that they are heading off the track. Even though it does not necessarily inform them in what way their path deviates from the expected, it does inform them that there is a need to adjust their language in some way. Further encounters may provide the positive evidence needed to highlight what constitutes an appropriate path and may thus enable learners to match language form and pragmatic intent.

In sum, we have provided both micro- and macro-analyses of non-native refusals and have suggested ways in which these difficult encounters may provide a basis for learning.

Appendices

Appendix I

Situations

1. You are ready to leave the house to go to a party with the children of your host family — Nathan, age 21, and Jennifer, age 23. They are telling you about their friends and the things they usually do at parties. The more they talk, the more you realize that everyone at the party will be using dangerous drugs. Nathan picks up his car keys and starts for the door [Invitation]

2. You are at your host family's home. Your host family, the Quentins, has gone to a neighbor's house to discuss a business matter. They have left you at home with specific instructions not to let anyone in the house, no matter what they say. It could be dangerous. About 5 minutes after they leave, the doorbell rings. It is a woman who says that she is Mr. Quentin's cousin from Detroit. She is just passing through Lansing and says, "Can I come in and wait?" [Request]

3. It is Saturday morning at your host family's home. At breakfast the family tells you that they have made reservations at the airport for all of you to go sky-diving this morning. The whole family — Mr. and Mrs. Cousins, Meg, and Tim — are all getting ready to go. They ask you if you have every gone skydiving before. When you say no, they say, "Don't worry! It's easy!" [Invitation]

4. It is Sunday morning and you have agreed to attend church services with your host family, the Jarvises. As you are getting ready to leave the house for church, Mrs. Jarvis informs you that there are plans for you to give a short speech about university life in Japan after the services. She says, "I hope you won't mind." [Request]

5. It is 11:00am Saturday morning at the home of your host family, the Larsons. You arrived at the Larsons' home last night at about 8:00pm. You thought that you would be having dinner with them, but they thought you had eaten, so you had no dinner. This morning you had only a piece of toast and coffee. You are now very hungry. Mrs. Larson walks into the room and tells you that you will be going to an

early barbecue for dinner. She suggests that because you will be eating at about 5:00pm, you skip lunch today. But you are really hungry. [Suggestion]

6. You are at the home of your host family, the Sumners. Both the children, Charlie and Karen Sumner, have short, very ugly haircuts. At one point, they ask you how you like their hair. You answer politely that it looks very cool and comfortable. Mrs. Sumner announces proudly that she cuts their hair herself. And because you like the style, she will be glad to cut your hair to look like theirs. "Now where are my scissors...?", she asks. [Offer]

7. You are watching MTV with your host family on Saturday. You notice that both men and women rock stars have at least 4 earrings in their ears. You comment that this style is very interesting. Your host family's son Bob, age 22, says, "Oh, I'm glad you like it. My girlfriend pierced my ears. Why don't you get yours done, too? I'll call her right now, and she can be here in 20 minutes to pierce your ears." Bob goes to the telephone to call. [Suggestion]

8. You are at your host family's home. Your host mother, Mrs. Boulware, is admiring the expensive new pen that your family gave you before you left Japan. Mrs. Boulware sets the pen down on a low table, and you and she go into the backyard to look at her flowers. When you return to the room, the Boulware's pet dog, Ruffy, is happily chewing on your pen. When Mrs. Boulware gets the pen out of Ruffy's mouth, it is ruined. Mrs. Boulware says, "Oh, I am so sorry. I'll buy you a new one." [Offer]

Appendix II

Transcription conventions

Spelling

Normal spelling is used for the NNSs and, with a few exceptions, ("y'd" for "you'd"; "c'n" for "can") for the NS.

Intonation/Punctuation

Utterances do not begin with capital letters; normal punctuation conventions are not followed; instead, intonation (usually at the end of a clause or a phrase) is indicated as follows:
At the end of a word, phrase, or clause
?   Rising Intonation
.   Falling Intonation
,   "Nonfinal Intonation" (usually a slight rise)
No punctuation at clause end indicates transcriber uncertainty

Other

(?) or ( )	incomprehensible word or phrase
(all right)	a word or phrase within parentheses indicates that the transcriber is not certain that s/he has heard the word or phrase correctly
[	indicates overlapping speech; it begins at the point at which the overlap occurs
=	means that the utterance on one line continues without pause where the next = sign picks it up (latches)
y-	a hyphen after an initial sound indicates a false start
(.)	a dot within parentheses indicates a brief pause
((laugh))	nonlinguistic occurrences such as laughter, sighs, that are not essential to the analysis are enclosed within double parentheses

CAPITALS	capital letters are used for nonverbal information important to the analysis (e.g., nods, gestures, shifts in posture or position).
LH	left hand
RH	right hand
NOD	refers to one nod
NODS	refers to more than one nod
NODS---	refers to nodding accompanying speech, with hyphens indicating how long the nodding (or other behavior) continues
HS	refers to one head shake
HSs	refers to more than one head shake;
HSs---	refers to head shakes accompanying speech, with hyphens indicating how long the head shaking continues

NOTE: If a nod or head shake does not accompany speech, it is indicated before or after the speech that it precedes or follows; if it accompanies speech, it is represented on a separate line beneath the speech it accompanies. Other nonverbal information is positioned below the speech with which it co-occurs.

Appendix III

Transcript

Greeting	NS: oh hi how are you doing
	NNS: oh fine thank you
	[
(Background to	NS: is uh is uh Quentin in
Request)	
	NNS: no uh no I'm not
	NS: no he's not in
	[
	NNS: uh no no he's not in
	NS: ahh where'd he go
	NNS: ahh he goes to neighbor (house)
	[
	NS: ah well
	do you mind if - I'm I'm his cousin
	and I'm just passing through Lansing
	tonight
	NNS: mm

	NS: and I'm I'm on my way to Detroit I'm
	on a on a business trip
	NNS: mm
REQUEST 1	NS: and and uh I'd like to see him I've got
	about half an hour or so | would you
	mind if I come in and wait for a minute
	or so an a til he comes back
Direct "no"	NNS: ah no wait wait I'm a guest to uh this
Reason a	home the- I can't uh I don't uh uh um I
Reason b	can't I don't know what uh I do this
	situation then ah
Request for Clarific.	NS: I'm sorry?
Clarific. of Reason b	NNS: uh he he don't tell me uh
	NS: ahh
	NNS: if another person come in his home
Rejection of Reason b	NS: yeah yeah but I I I'm his cousin I'm=

	NS: =sure it's going to be ok=
	[
	NNS: but
Repetition of Reason b/(or begin Reason c)	NNS: =((laughs)) I don't know=
Repetition of Rejection of b	NS: =I I know it'll be all right=
Reason c	NNS: =my first time to meet you. I don't know you
Response to Reason c	NS: y'know actually this is the first time I've met you too how do you do=
	[
	NNS: wait wait
	NS: =nice to meet you
	[
Reason for Alternative 1	I think uh I think uh he came back uh not so late=
Alternative 1	NNS: ((slightly louder)) uh huh yeh uh please wait uh your car
(Reaction) (=Reject Alternative 1)	NS: ((gasps))
	NNS: ((slightly louder)) uh uh if you want to meet uh
(Reaction cont.)	NS: I can't believe this
	[
	NNS: him
Reason for Reaction/ Rejection	NS: I can't believe this this is my cousin this is my cousin
	[
Restatement of Reason c	NNS: but I don't know you
	[
	NS: we grew up together we went fishing together
	NNS: uh
Statement of Refusal Implication	NS: you mean to tell me I can't even come in his house
Restatement of Reason c	NNS: (but) I don't know you are cousin I don't know

Challenge (=Rejection · of Reason c)	NS:	well who uh a- a- a- a- a- uh- uh- that's not my problem
	NNS:	oh yeah
(Rejection cont.)	NS:	that's not my problem you don't know? what do you what are you=
	NNS:	nn
Reason for Rejection of c	NS:	talking about this is this is Quentin's my cousin what are you doing
	NNS:	oohnn
Statement of Refusal Implication	NS:	you're not going to let me in his house=
(Reaction)	NNS:	uhh
	NS:	=I can't believe this
Reason d	NNS:	I said it's my business I now I homestay yeh I cannot door open
Challenge (=Rejection of Reason d)	NS:	what do you mean it's your business who are you how do I know you're not a burglar
Denial	NNS:	no
Complaint (=Threat)	NS:	I'm a oh boy boy Quentin's not going to hear the last of this
REQUEST 2		come on let me in
	NNS:	aoo
Reason for Request	NS:	come on I've been traveling all the way from Muskegon
	NNS:	oh yeah
Repetition of Request	NS:	and I was win in Chi- Chicago the night before I'm beat let me in let me sit down and wait for Quentin this is ridiculous
	NNS:	ahh so

Regret **Reason e**	I feel very sorry yeah but I so I cannot decide this door open
REQUEST 3	NS: |oh come on
	NNS: yeah
	NS: just let me in
	NNS: yeah uh
	NS: just yeh let me in
Alternative 2	NNS: yeah oh so ah I think you had better to go neighbor's house to uh to meet him
Req for Clarification re Alternative 2/Complaint	NS: oh Quentin oh wh wh what neighbor's house is he at boy he's not going to= [
Apology	NNS: excuse excuse me=
Response to Request for Clarification	NS: =hear the last of this NNS: =I don't know
Request for Confirmation	NS: you don't know whe-
Confirmation	NNS: yeah
(Reaction)	NS: aiiii
Elaboration of Response to Request for Confirm.	NNS: but not so far from (here) maybe I (near the house) [
(Sarcastic) Request for Clarification (Sincere) Response to Request for Clarification	NS: so what am I supposed to do drive around? I don't know his neighbors either NNS: uh y-you can uh go by walk

(Sarcastic) Thanks	NS:	thank you thank you very much very kind of=

               [[[

(Sincere)   NNS: yeah   yeah   yeah
Acknowledgment

Situation Summary   NS: =you. I've driven f- 13 hours and I can walk around in the neighborhood and y- I don't know where I'm looking I don't know who t- whose house to go to

                                [

NNS: but

REQUEST 4   NS: |come on come on just let me in let me in=

                                  [

NNS: ahhh

Reason for Request   NS: =let me sit down and take it easy and rest for a while I'm thirsty

                    [

NNS: ahm

Acknowledgment   NNS: yeah

Confirmation   NS: yeah

Expression of Empathy   NNS: it's a problem

Confirmation   NS: yeah it's a problem

Expression of Empathy   NNS: uh it's a problem

Reason for Request   NS: I'm tired I'm beat

Acknowledgment   NNS: umm yeah
REQUEST 5   NS: let me in an n let me sit uh come in and sit down and wait

Reasons e and b for Refusal   NNS: but I can't decide uh you come in ( ) I I can't do that uh I can't what I do this situation (I can't do)

(Reaction)
Acceptance of Refusal   NS: ((sighs)) ah huh huh I don't believe it ok all right ok all right when ya when ya tell

Complaint/Farewell

when you see Quentin tell him he's a son
of a gun ok
((NS leaves))

Notes

1. As we will discuss in greater detail in Chapter Two, this is an area that is frequently missed by the use of the most commonly used data elicitation measure — discourse completion tests.
2. This definition is an oversimplification since, as we will show in later chapters, negotiation is not exclusively linguistic. In other words, more than just linguistic acts are often involved.
3. Note that putting off is not the same as postponing. A put-off is temporary; postponement, if effective, functions as a Final Outcome until the issue is reopened on another occasion.
4. The dialogues consisted of two parts — an initiating act by, for example, a requester, followed by a space for a refusal. There was then a follow-up request, followed by a space for a further refusal.
5. Ueda went on to analyze the results in greater detail according to the approaches preferred by members of older or younger groups and by men or women.
6. Semantic formulas are a pragmatic notion referring to "the means by which a particular speech act is accomplished in terms of the primary content of an utterance....a superset of specific content" (Bardovi-Harlig and Hartford 1991: 48).
7. An alternative to detailed ethnographic data is what Beebe (1994) refers to as "notebook data". The collection procedure for this data type consists of observing and memorizing the core act (e.g., refusal) when it occurs, as well as any supporting moves that the researcher can commit to memory; writing down immediately everything that the researcher can recall precisely, as well as any partially recalled speech or additional information that may be relevant to a description of the interaction; in addition, researchers must make notes being careful to reflect which dialogue was recalled verbatim and which was reconstructed. Although it is limited to capturing short interactions, the method allows an alert observer to gather large amounts of data on particular types of acts in relatively short spans of time.
8. Cohen (1996) and Cohen and Olshtain (1993) have discussed the issue of triangulation, highlighting the need to validate findings by means of various elicitation types.
9. The focus on discourse completion tests and role plays is intended to reflect the fact that these two methodologies are and continue to be predominant ones in speech act research. Others exist although they

will not be dealt with in this discussion of research methodologies. For example, Robinson (1992) investigated pragmatic competence by means of introspection, with an emphasis on language processing, combining discourse completion test data with verbal report data. Robinson found difficulties with the former, such as an inability to picture settings and interlocutors and a preference for acceptance of requests and invitations. Through verbal reports from subjects, Robinson was able to add a richness of information to our knowledge of speech acts by documenting utterance planning, evaluations of alternative utterance possibilities, pragmatic and linguistic difficulties, and misunderstandings of discourse completion tests in general.

10. The eliciting instrument was based on Scarcella's conceptualization of socio-drama (1978).

11. This may, of course, be due to the instructions given to the participants, but also may be a result of the methodology used, a methodology that did not allow for a comfortable closure early on in the interaction.

12. Clearly, the result is messy. In our data, the elicitation instrument determined the nature of the initiating speech act but had no real effect on the remaining speech; in pure observational research, the researcher controls even less (cf. Beebe 1993).

13. These figures should be treated as relative estimates since, particularly among learners of lower English ability, it was often difficult to establish what constituted a turn.

14. In addition to the native speaker's persistence, it might be expected that the amount of negotiation reflected a Japanese reluctance to refuse directly. However, a look at the non-native speakers' use of the most direct linguistic refusal *no* indicates that they were often willing to state refusals directly. (In five of the eight role plays, the Japanese subjects indicated refusal at least once with *no*.) This is corroborated by data from Kinjo (1987) and Rose (1994), who found that Japanese subjects were more direct than the American subjects.

    The data from this study indicate that Japanese subjects will give direct negative responses, at least in some situations. A study of the factors responsible for determining the level of directness is outside the scope of this book.

15. As Joyce Neu (personal communication) points out, there are other interpretations possible to a phrase such as "But I don't know you." For example, it may be challenge to the speaker's right to ask the hearer to do X (as in Beebe, Takahashi, and Uliss-Weltz's 1990: 75 subcategory "Criticize the request/requester"). While this might be

the case in interactions between two native speakers, we are confident that in our data, given the participants, given the intonation, and given the posture and facial expressions, these are sincere reasons/explanations.

16. Line numbers are given for easy identification of a particular point in the discourse and are not intended to make any theoretical claim regarding the nature of the talk thereby identified.

17. Bardovi-Harlig and Hartford (1990) have pointed out that requests for information are employed by non-native speakers as an indirect means of avoiding a refusal, in their case a refusal of a suggestion. The interaction in Example (7) took place after the meaning of skydiving had been carefully explained and after a previous role play on skydiving had been acted out in front of the non-native speaker.

    Interestingly, another non-native speaker, who had observed two skydiving role plays, also requested an explanation of the term skydiving during his own skydiving role play, supporting the contention that these requests for clarification may reflect the speaker's wish to avoid direct refusal rather than a real need to negotiate meaning.

18. Our notion of episode is also similar to Edmondson's (1981) *exchange*, an interactional structure composed of *moves*.

19. Of course, these resources are often based on first language formulas, as Beebe, Takahashi, and Uliss-Weltz (1990) have shown. Our point is that their choice of semantic formulas over a series of episodes involves more than a non-native speaker's simple selection of a semantic formula from the set of formulas that would be suitable in the first language.

20. Beebe, Takahashi, and Uliss-Weltz (1990) found that Japanese used fewer "no"s in response to offers from interlocutors of all status, more statements of regret in request and offer refusals to higher status requesters and offerers, and fewer statements of regret in invitation refusals to lower status inviters. Throughout the interaction we are reporting, the Japanese non-native speaker resorted more to the semantic formulas that Beebe, Takahashi, and Uliss-Weltz found to be associated with refusals to higher or equal status rather than lower status Japanese interlocutors.

21. We have classified non-native speaker expressions of ignorance as a reason (or excuse) for noncompliance in Beebe, Takahashi, and Uliss-Weltz's (1990) system, rather than as an instance of a hedge indicating avoidance, since the expression of ignorance seems to be functioning in this situation as a part of a the non-native speaker's global reason for refusing (I'm a guest who doesn't know who you

are or what to do in this situation and who cannot decide), and since the non-native speaker makes it clear throughout that a refusal is intended.

22. In doing so, he manages to keep his semantic content consistent (unlike Bardovi-Harlig and Hartford's [1991] non-native speakers, who sometimes offered contradictory reasons for their refusals).

23. Of course, as Yngve (1970) points out, the term *listener* is not really appropriate, as in uttering back channels, the "listener" is speaking.

24. In this chapter, we are primarily concerned with transition fillers that do not result in a change of turn.

25. Within the acquisition literature this is discussed under the concept of Indirect Negative Evidence. The interested reader is referred to Plough (1994, 1996).

26. In fact, such comments are included as back channels in earlier definitions of back channels such as those of Yngve (1970) and Duncan and Niederehe (1974).

27. The coordination of a nod with an agreeing negative is not an impossibility in native speaker English interaction. However, it requires a certain sophistication in terms of intonation, tone, and volume that we are at this stage reluctant to attribute to a low proficiency non-native speaker.

28. The inclusion of verbalizations and nods at points where the speaker does not pause is a departure from Maynard.

29. In this study we consider only the nature of the current interaction in our discussion of back channel frequency during refusal negotiations. However, we note that frequency of occurrence can be influenced not only by the course of the interaction, but also by the non-native speaker's interactional style. For instance, Hayashi (1990) has pointed out that large individual differences in back channel frequencies exist among Japanese speakers.

30. In Clancy, Thompson, Suzuki, and Tao's (1996) classification system, these phrases would probably be classified as *reactive expressions*, rather than back channels.

31. Note that differences in back channel use do not necessarily lead to problems or misunderstandings in cross-cultural interactions. For instance, although Japanese have been reported to use minimal vocalizations and nods to a greater extent and for different purposes than do most native speakers of English, according to S. White (1989), they are perceived by native speakers of English not as inappropriate, but rather as more patient, polite and attentive conversational partners than native speakers. Americans also evaluated those Japanese lis-

teners who produced more back channels as more encouraging, concerned, and interested than those who produced fewer. It appears
that, at least in some circumstances, this use of back channels by
English-speaking Japanese fosters positive feelings in Americans.

32. A similar phenomenon has been pointed out by Maltz and Borker
(1982). They hypothesize that for women minimal responses mean
something like "I'm listening to you please continue", whereas for
men the meaning is stronger, something like "I agree with you" or "I
follow your argument so far" (p. 202).

33. Many are certainly aware of the differences between *yeah* or *yes* and
Japanese *hai*. An advanced Japanese non-native speaker of English
in Tokyo informed us that she often used Japanese *hai* as a back
channel in situations where it would be appropriate in Japanese when
speaking English to native speakers because she is uncomfortable
with the choices of English back channels.

34. Even when it cannot be construed as agreement to perform some act,
as in LoCastro's case, the use of *yeah* to perform a primary vocalization when another response (in this case an apology) might be more
appropriate can be confusing and potentially insulting.

35. See Kawate-Mierzejewska (1997) for a discussion of problems aris-
ing from the misuse of Japanese back channels by a non-native
speaker of English conversing in Japanese.

36. Patterson (1994) notes that "characterizing strategic patterns as deliberate and managed does not mean that the actor necessarily has
awareness of what he or she is doing during a strategic display.
Well-learned or scripted influence attempts may be initiated automatically when situation [*sic*] calls for it. Nevertheless, these auto-
matic displays would be deliberate and managed in their origin. That
is, in learning such patterns, actors have some awareness of their intention and, in most cases, awareness of their behavior" (p. 289).

37. An important point to make here is that claims about the associations
between particular nonverbal behaviors and impressions conveyed by
these behaviors rely heavily on research involving members of English-speaking cultures (primarily in the U.S. and Canada). As such,
they represent the expectations and impressions of members of specific English-speaking communities. In addition, functions and interpretations of nonverbal behavior can be affected by changes in context.

38. Because this chapter deals with a comparison of three speakers, to
distinguish the participants more clearly, we have assigned a ficti-
tious name to each of them. Also, as mentioned, a number of ges-

tures are included in the transcripts. Note that, with a few exceptions, only the non-native speaker's gestures are described. Gestures to items such as a TV or telephone refer to gestures to imaginary props.

39. See Ekman and Friesen (1969) for a discussion of the types of meaning conveyed by individual adjustments in, for example, facial expression and posture.

40. It appears that Ryo is attempting a causative passive construction ("I don't want to be pierced (.) my ears" = I don't want to have my ears pierced), undoubtedly a difficult syntactic structure in English.

41. When videotapes of the three non-native speakers were shown to native speakers of Japanese, they agreed that the nonverbal behavior of all three Japanese was polite and appropriate for the situation, albeit for different reasons. When the tapes were shown to native speakers of English, several of the viewers felt that Ryo's gestures conveyed aggression. The Japanese viewers strongly disagreed.

42. Kitao (1997) cites Kim's (1994) research indicating that members of different cultures may weigh conversational constraints differently. For instance, members of collectivist cultures such as Japan may weigh concern not to hurt the hearer's feelings and not to impose on the hearer much higher than members of individualist cultures such as the U.S., which value effectiveness more highly. Thus, it would not be surprising to find that the three Japanese non-native speakers of English in these role plays were using nonlinguistic resources to make their refusals as inoffensive as possible.

43. It is of course quite possible that, despite participants' claims that they would have stopped attempting to refuse and accepted even had the situation been a real-life one, the large percentage of acceptances is a result of the fact that the situation was a role play and had no real-life consequences.

44. Unsurprisingly, proficiency level seemed to be associated with the degree of negotiation, with more proficient speakers sometimes attempting to negotiate more.

45. In fact, it may also reveal that the goal of the non-native speaker was not a refusal, as it might initially appear, but some solution that allowed the native speaker and the non-native speaker to do something jointly. In this case, the result was an acceptance with conditions.

46. These differences may be influenced by the specific request, invitation, offer, or suggestion, by general cultural values, or by individual differences. We are not in a position to put forth an opinion as to which were operating in our data.

47. The lack of non-native speaker volubility in the data may be a consequence of the elicitation instrument. The paucity of long non-native speaker turns in the data is sometimes a result of the fact that the native speaker begins to talk at the first opportunity making it difficult for non-native speakers to talk at length even if they had wanted to. And in fact, Edmondson and House (1991) note that this behavior may be associated with the use of discourse completion tests, as on a discourse completion test the respondent does not have access to the hearer's reaction, nor is she vulnerable to interruption.

48. This is particularly true of the lower proficiency non-native speakers in the study.

49. Tannen notes that not only speakers of different languages, but even speakers of the same language with different dialects or conversational styles may come to a conversation with different expectations.

50. Halmari (1993) notes a similar phenomenon. She presents an example of a Finnish man who had been conducting business in the United States for many years but who was still accustomed to using the Finnish business practice of including a long non-business related discussion prior to entering into the business part of the conversation. This is exemplified below (Halmari, 1993: 416-417)

   1 NS: Okay. How are you doing today?
   2 NNS: I'm real bad. I was so- w-we have been SO angry with my wife because we have problems with the computer.
   3 NS: (laughs) hah-hah-hah-hah-ha!
   4 NNS: You don't believe how how these people how they are-er they are sending us to four different companies. I never buy an EB- IBM any more.
   5 NS: Oh REALLY?
   6 NNS: Yeah
   7 NS: You have a big problem with your IBM?
   8 NNS: Ye:s
   9 NS: How funny.
 10 NNS: Yeah and I think that it is the basically that the first guy who sold it to us he put the wrong serial number in the guarantee papers.
 11 NS: O:h.
           [
 12 NNS: We have a warranty on it but the serial number is different. He has made a m-smesh to us and it's going to cost almost two thousand DOLLARS.

13 NS: Oh N:O!
            [
14 NNS: So I'm pissed.
15 NS: I- I would be very pissed too hah|-hah!
16 NNS: |Yeah.
17 NS: O:h what an awful thing that-s that's a lot of cars you
           have to sell.
18 NNS: Yeah. I have to ship a many many many cars.
19 NS: That's a lot of cars for a lousy computer.
20 NNS: Yes (laughs)
21 NS: Same for me too.
22 NNS: Oh?
23 NS   SO. I'm returning your call regarding a RATE that you
           want.

As can be seen, the native speaker only minimally engages in the
conversation (lines 3, 5, 9, 11, 13). He began the conversation with a
perfunctory "How are you doing today?" to which he undoubtedly
expected only a limited answer. In fact, in line 17, it appears that he
started (unsuccessfully) to bridge to a business context. However,
perhaps because the Finnish man expected to be engaged in a lengthy
mutual non-topical discussion, he did not pick up on the segue into
the business purpose of the call.

51. As discussed in Chapter One, an outcome can have a number of
     forms.

52. We do not wish to imply that there is in any sense a predictable script
     or predetermined list of responses which the native speaker expects
     the non-native speaker to follow. Rather we are claiming that, in a
     particular "culture" and situation (social and discourse), given a move
     by a conversationalist, there will be a possibly very large set of re-
     sponses that will be perceived as unexceptional and interpretable.
     There will be a probably even larger set of (usually unrealized) re-
     sponses that would register as exceptional or uninterpretable and that
     would require some work to make them interpretable to a member of
     the culture.

53. Of course the need for an explanation will be situation and person
     dependent.

54. In our data with more advanced non-native speakers, inappropriate
     content also received marked reactions from the native speaker. Af-
     ter one inappropriate counterproposal, a native speaker reacted with
     shock; after another, with sarcasm (See Chapter 3).

55. Obviously there are other things going on in this interaction than the native speaker's attempt to reestablish that the non-native speaker likes her children's haircuts. For instance, the non-native speaker's lack of response is not explained. Among other things, it may be a result of the pacing of the native speaker's repetitions, which might not allow the non-native speaker the time he needs to formulate a response or to request clarification. Thus, the non-native speaker's *uh* and *um* may be a prelude to speech, a need to buy time, or an indication of confusion, rather than an attempt to pass on an opportunity to talk. Also, the native speaker's intention in restating may originally be simply to elicit elaboration from the non-native speaker. However, when the native speaker does not confirm this presumably previously established proposition, the native speaker needs to check on its status in the discourse before proceeding on the assumption that it is shared.

56. Hatch (1978) has reported a similar phenomenon when non-native speakers attempt to establish a topic. She notes that "Perhaps because the nominations and comments are so lengthy, the native speaker seems driven to paraphrase everything that has been said in one sentence. This occurs in all the data we've looked at for adults" (p.426). Hatch views the native speaker's paraphrase as an attempt to reassure the non-native speaker that s/he has been understood. This may indeed be the purpose of native speaker repetitions/paraphrases in some of our data; however, in many instances, establishment of the repeated or paraphrased utterance or proposition as part of the shared discourse is also essential before the native speaker can make her next move toward reaching a mutually agreed upon outcome.

57. See Pinker (1994: 277-278) for a discussion of the irrelevance of this dichotomy. He takes the position that the nature/nurture argument is a false dichotomy. He makes the point that if wild children "...had run out of the woods speaking Phrygian or ProtoWorld, who could they have talked to? (1994: 277). In other words, nature provides part of the answer and nurture provides another.

58. Empty Category Principle.

59. In *wh*-questions, movement is involved in which the *wh*-word is moved from its underlying position to the front of the sentence. When this occurs, a trace (*t*) is left in the original position. The existence of this trace has important consequences for later syntactic operations (see Gass 1997).

60. The arguments are in actuality far more complex and include issues of awareness (see Gass 1997 for additional discussion).

61. We are aware that there may be circumstances, such as an emergency in which the particular book in question might contain life-saving information, in which a direct request might not be rude at all, but might instead represent the norm.
62. We confess to falling into this same trap, at times referring to the participants in our study as "non-native speakers" and at other times referring to them as "learners."

References

Andersen, Roger and Yas Shirai
    1996   The primacy of aspect in first and second language acqui-
              sition: The pidgin-creole connection. In: William Ritchie
              and Taj Bhatia (eds.), *Handbook of Second Language Ac-*
              quisition, 527-570. San Diego: Academic Press.

Archibald, John
    1993   Indirect negative evidence and blame assignment in L2
              parameter setting. Paper presented at the University of
              Wisconsin-Milwaukee Linguistics Symposium, Milwau-
              kee, October.

Aston, Guy
    1993   Notes on the interlanguage of comity. In: Gabriele Kasper
              and Shoshana Blum-Kulka (eds.), *Interlanguage Prag-*
              matics, 224-250. New York: Oxford University Press.

Austin, John L.
    1975   *How to Do Things with Words* (2nd edition). Cambridge,
              MA: Harvard University Press.

Bachman, Lyle
    1990   *Fundamental Considerations in Language Testing.* Ox-
              ford: Oxford University Press.

Bachman, Lyle and Adrian Palmer
    1996   *Language Testing in Practice.* Oxford: Oxford University
              Press.

Bardovi-Harlig, Kathleen
    1998   Exploring the interlanguage of interlanguage pragmatics:
              A research agenda for acquisitional pragmatics. Paper
              presented at the Second Language Research Forum,
              Honolulu, October.

Bardovi-Harlig, Kathleen and Zoltán Dörnyei
    1998   Do language learners recognize pragmatic violations?
              Pragmatic versus grammatial awareness in instructed L2
              learning. *TESOL Quarterly* 32: 233-262.

Bardovi-Harlig, Kathleen and Beverly Hartford
    1990   Learning to say 'no': Native and non-native rejections in
              English. Paper presented at the Conference on Pragmatics
              and Language Learning, Urbana-Champaign, April.

1991   Saying 'no' in English: Native and nonnative rejections.
            In: Lawrence Bouton and Yamuna Kachru (eds.), *Prag-
            matics and Language Learning 2*, 41-58.   Urbana-
            Champaign, IL: University of Illinois.

1992   Natural conversations, institutional talk, and interlanguage
            pragmatics. Paper presented at the Pacific Second Lan-
            guage Research Forum, Sydney, July.

1993   Learning the rules of academic talk: A longitudinal study
            of pragmatic change. *Studies in Second Language Acqui-
            sition* 15: 279-304.

1996   Input in an institutional setting. *Studies in Second Lan-
            guage Acquisition* 18: 171-188.

Beebe, Leslie

1993   Rudeness: The neglected side of communicative compe-
            tence? Paper presented at the TESOL (Teachers of English
            to Speakers of Other Languages) Sociolinguistics Collo-
            quium, Atlanta, April.

1994   Notebook data on power and the power of notebook data.
            Paper presented at the TESOL (Teachers of English to
            Speakers of Other Languages) Sociolinguistics Collo-
            quium, Baltimore, March.

Beebe, Leslie and Martha Cummings

1985   Speech act performance: A function of the data collection
            procedure. Paper presented at the TESOL (Teachers of
            English to Speakers of Other Languages) Sociolinguistics
            Colloquium, New York, April.

1996   Natural speech act data versus written questionnaire data:
            How data collection method affects speech act perform-
            ance. In: Susan Gass and Joyce Neu (eds.), *Speech Acts
            across Cultures: Challenges to Communication in a Sec-
            ond Language,* 65-86. Berlin: Mouton de Gruyter.

Beebe, Leslie, Tomoko Takahashi and Robin Uliss-Weltz

1990   Pragmatic transfer in ESL refusals. In: Robin Scarcella,
            Elaine Andersen and Stephen Krashen (eds.), *Developing
            Communicative Competence in a Second Language*, 55-
            73. New York: Newbury House.

Bialystok, Ellen

1990   *Communication Strategies: A Psychological Analysis of
            Second-Language Use.* Oxford: Basil Blackwell.

Birdsong, David
1989 *Metalinguistic Performance and Interlinguistic Competence.* Berlin: Springer Verlag.

Bley-Vroman, Robert
1987 The fundamental character of foreign language learning. In: William Rutherford and Michael Sharwood Smith (eds.), *Grammar and Second Language Teaching*, 19-30. Rowley, MA: Newbury House.

Bloomfield, Leonard
1933 *Language.* New York: Holt, Rinehart, and Winston.

Blum-Kulka, Shoshana, Juliane House and Gabriele Kasper (eds.)
1989 *Cross-cultural Pragmatics: Requests and Apologies.* Norwood, NJ: Ablex.

Blum-Kulka, Shoshana and Elite Olshtain
1984 Requests and apologies: A cross-cultural study of speech act realization patterns. *Applied Linguistics* 7: 196-213.
1986 Too many words: length of utterance and pragmatic failure. *Studies in Second Language Acquisition* 8: 165-180.

Canale, Michael
1983 From communicative competence to communicative language pedagogy. In: Jack Richards and Richard Schmidt (eds.), *Language and Communication*, 3-27. London: Longman.

Cazden, Courtney
1972 *Child Language and Education.* New York: Holt, Rinehart and Winston.

Celce-Murcia, Marianne, Zoltán Dörnyei and Sarah Thurrell
1995 Communicative competence: A pedagogically motivated model with content specifications. *Issues in Applied Linguistics* 6: 5-35.

Chaudron, Craig
in prep. *Elicited Imitation.* Mahwah, N.J.: Lawrence Erlbaum Associates.

Chen, Xing, Lei Ye and Yanyin Zhang
1995 Refusing in Chinese. In: Gabriele Kasper (ed.), *Pragmatics of Chinese as Native and Target Language* (Technical Report #5), 119-163. Manoa, HI: University of Hawai'i Press.

Chomsky, Noam
1980 *Rules and Representations.* New York: Columbia University Press.

1987   Kyoto Lectures, unpublished ms.

Clancy, Patricia, Sandra Thompson, Ryoko Suzuki and Hongyin Tao
1996   The conversational use of reactive tokens in English, Japanese, and Mandarin. *Journal of Pragmatics* 26: 355-387.

Cohen, Andrew
1996   Investigating the production of speech act sets. In: Susan Gass and Joyce Neu (eds.), *Speech Acts across Cultures: Challenges to Communication in a Second Language*, 21-43. Berlin: Mouton de Gruyter.

Cohen, Andrew and Elite Olshtain
1993   The production of speech acts by EFL learners. *TESOL Quarterly* 27: 33-56.
1994   Researching the production of speech acts. In: Elaine Tarone, Susan Gass and Andrew Cohen (eds.), *Research Methodology in Second Language Acquisition*, 143-155. Hillsdale, NJ: Lawrence Erlbaum Associates.

Cook, Vivian
1988   *Chomsky's Universal Grammar*. Oxford: Basil Blackwell.
1993   *Linguistics and Second Language Acquisition*. London: MacMillan Press.

Corder, S. Pit
1977   Simple codes and the source of the second language learner's initial heuristic hypothesis. *Studies in Second Language Acquisition* 1: 1-10.

Duff, Patsy
in prep.   *Case Studies in Second Language Acquisition Research*. Mahwah, NJ: Lawrence Erlbaum Associates.

Duncan, Starkey
1973   On the structure of speaker-auditor interaction during speaking turns. *Language in Society* 2: 161-180.

Duncan, Starkey and George Niederehe
1974   On signaling that it's your turn to speak. *Journal of Social Psychology* 10: 234-247.

Edmondson, Willis
1981   *Spoken Discourse: A Model for Analysis*. London: Longman.

Edmondson, Willis and Juliane House
1991   Do learners talk too much? The waffle phenomenon in interlanguage pragmatics. In: Robert Phillipson, Eric Kellerman, Larry Selinker, Michael Sharwood Smith and

Merrill Swain (eds.), *Foreign/Second Language Pedagogy Research,* 273-286. Clevedon, UK: Multilingual Matters.

Ekman, Paul
1978   Facial expression. In: Aron Siegman and Stanley Feldstein (eds.), *Nonverbal Behavior and Communication,* 97-116. New York: John Wiley & Sons.

Ekman, Paul and Wallace Friesen
1969   The repertoire of nonverbal behavior: Categories, origins, usage, and coding. *Semiotica* 1: 49-98.

Ellis, Rod
1994   *The Study of Second Language Acquisition.* Oxford: Oxford University Press.

Erickson, Frederick and Jeffrey Shultz
1982   *The Counselor as Gatekeeper: Social Interaction in Interviews.* New York: Academic Press.

Færch, Claus and Gabriele Kasper
1983a   On identifying communication strategies in interlanguage production. In: Claus Faerch and Gabriele Kasper (eds.), *Strategies in Interlanguage Communication,* 210-238. London: Longman.

1983b   Plans and strategies in foreign language communication. In: Claus Færch and Gabriele Kasper (eds.), *Strategies in Interlanguage Communication,* 20-60. London: Longman.

1987   From product to process — Introspective methods in second language research. In: Claus Færch and Gabriele Kasper (eds.), *Introspection in Second Language Research,* 5-23. Clevedon, U.K.: Multilingual Matters.

Fiksdal, Susan
1990   *The Right Time and Pace: A Microanalysis of Cross-cultural Gatekeeping Interviews.* Norwood, NJ: Ablex.

Gass, Susan
1984   A review of interlanguage syntax: Language transfer and language universals. *Language Learning* 34: 115-132.

1988   Integrating research areas: A framework for second language studies. *Applied Linguistics* 9: 198-217.

1994   The reliability of L2 grammaticality judgments. In: Elaine Tarone, Susan Gass and Andrew Cohen (eds.), *Research Methodology in Second Language Acquisition,* 303-322. Hillsdale, NJ: Lawrence Erlbaum Associates.

1995   Learning and teaching: The necessary intersection. In: Fred R. Eckman, Diane Highland, Peter W. Lee, Jean

Mileham and Rita Rutkowski Weber (eds.), *Second Language Acquisition Theory and Pedagogy,* 3-20. Mahwah, NJ: Lawrence Erlbaum Associates.

1997   *Input, Interaction and the Second Language Learner.* Mahwah, NJ: Lawrence Erlbaum Associates.

1998   Apples and oranges: Or, why apples are not oranges and don't need to be. *Modern Language Journal* 82: 83-90.

Gass, Susan and Josh Ard

1984   L2 acquisition and the ontology of language universals. In: William Rutherford (ed.), *Second Language Acquisition and Language Universals,* 33-68. Amsterdam: John Benjamins.

Gass, Susan and Alison Mackey

in prep.   *Stimulated Recall in Second Language Research.* Mahwah, NJ: Lawrence Erlbaum Associates.

Gass, Susan, Alison Mackey and Teresa Pica

1998   The role of input and interaction in second language acquisition. *Modern Language Journal* 82: 290-307.

Gass, Susan and Joyce Neu (eds.)

1996   *Speech Acts across Cultures: Challenges to Communication in a Second Language.* Berlin: Mouton de Gruyter.

Gass, Susan and Larry Selinker

1994   *Second Language Acquisition: An Introductory Course.* Hillsdale, NJ: Lawrence Erlbaum Associates.

Gass, Susan and Evangeline Varonis

1985   Task variation and nonnative/nonnative negotiation of meaning. In: Susan Gass and Carolyn Madden (eds.), *Input in Second Language Acquisition,* 149-178. Rowley, Mass: Newbury House.

1989   Incorporated repairs in nonnative discourse. In: Miriam Eisenstein (ed.), *The Dynamic Interlanguage: Empirical Studies in Second Language Variation,* 71-86. New York: Plenum Press.

1994   Input, interaction and second language production. *Studies in Second Language Acquisition* 16: 283-302

Goffman, Erving

1971   *Relations in Public: Microstudies of the Public Order.* New York: Basic Books.

Goodwin, Charles and Marjorie Goodwin
  1987   Concurrent operations on talk: Notes on the interactive or-
            ganization of assessments. *IPrA Papers in Pragmatics* 1:
            1-54.
Goss, Nancy, Ying-Hua Zhang and James Lantolf
  1994   Two heads may be better than one: Mental activity in sec-
            ond-language grammaticality judgments. In: Elaine
            Tarone, Susan Gass and Andrew Cohen (eds.), *Research
            Methodology in Second-Language Acquisition*, 263-286.
            Hillsdale, NJ: Lawrence Erlbaum Associates.
Gullberg, Marianne
  1998   *Gesture as a Communication Strategy in Second Lan-
            guage Discourse: A Study of Learners of French and
            Swedish.* Lund: Lund University Press
Gumperz, John
  1982   *Discourse Strategies.* New York: Cambridge University
            Press.
  1990   The conversational analysis of interethnic communication
            In: Robin Scarcella, Elaine Andersen and   Stephen
            Krashen (eds.), *Developing Communicative Competence
            in a Second Language*, 223-238. New York: Newbury
            House.
Gumperz, John, Thomas Jupp and Cecilia Roberts
  1979   *Crosstalk: A Study of Cross-cultural Communication.*
            London: The National Centre for Industrial Language
            Training.
Gumperz, John and Deborah Tannen
  1979   Individual and social differences in language use. In:
            Charles Fillmore, Daniel Kempler and William W.-Y.
            Wang (eds.), *Individual Differences in Language Ability
            and Language Behavior,* 305-325. New York: Academic
            Press.
Halmari, Helena
  1993   Intercultural business telephone conversations: A case of
            Finns vs. Anglo-Americans. *Applied Linguistics* 14: 408-
            430.
Harrington, Michael
  in prep. *Data-driven Modeling: The Competition Model.* Mahwah,
            NJ: Lawrence Erlbaum Associates.

Hartford, Beverly and Kathleen Bardovi-Harlig
    1992   Experimental and observational data in the study of inter-
                language pragmatics. In: Lawrence Bouton and Yamuna
                Kachru (eds.), *Pragmatics and Language Learning 3*, 33-
                52. Urbana-Champaign, IL: University of Illinois.
Hatch, Evelyn
    1978   Discourse analysis and second language acquisition. In:
                Evelyn Hatch (ed.), *Second Language Acquisition: A Book
                of Readings,* 410-435. Rowley, MA: Newbury House.
    1992   *Discourse and Language Education.* New York: Cam-
                bridge University Press.
Hayashi, Reiko
    1990   Rhythmicity sequence and synchrony of English and
                Japanese face-to-face conversation. *Language Sciences*
                12: 155-195.
Hayashi, Takuo and Reiko Hayashi
    1991   Back channel or main channel: A cognitive approach
                based on floor and speech acts. In: Lawrence Bouton and
                Yamuna Kachru (eds.), *Pragmatics and Language
                Learning 2*, 119-138. Urbana-Champaign, IL: University
                of Illinois.
Hinds, John
    1978   Conversational structure: An investigation based on Japa-
                nese interview discourse. In: John Hinds and I. Howard
                (eds.), *Problems in Japanese Syntax and Semantics,* 79-
                121. Tokyo: Kaitakusha Co. Ltd.
Houck, Noël
    1998   Pragmatic communication strategies. In: Taiji Fujimura,
                Yoko Kato and Richard Smith (ed.), *Proceedings of the 9th
                Conference on Second Language Research in Japan,* 34-
                55. Niigata: International University of Japan.
Houck, Noël and Susan Gass
    1996   Non-native refusals: A methodological perspective. In:
                Susan Gass and Joyce Neu (eds.), *Speech Acts across
                Cultures: Challenges to Communication in a Second Lan-
                guage,* 45-64. Berlin: Mouton de Gruyter.
    1997   Nonverbal communication in non-native refusals. In:
                Adam Jaworski (ed.), *Silence: Interdisciplinary Perspec-
                tives,* 285-308. Berlin: Mouton de Gruyter
    in press   Dancing a waltz to rock & roll music: Resolving conflict-
                ing discourse expectations in cross-cultural interaction.

In: Jacek Fisiak (ed.), *Festschrift for Kari Sajavaara on his sixtieth birthday (Studia Anglica Posnaniensia 33)*, 131-140. Poznan: Wydawnictwo Nakom.

Hudson, Thom, Emily Detmer and James D. Brown
1992   *A Framework for Testing Cross-cultural Pragmatics.* (Technical Report #2.) Manoa, HI: University of Hawai'i Press.
1995   *Developing Prototypic Measures of Cross-cultural Pragmatics.* (Technical Report #7.) Manoa, HI: University of Hawai'i Press.

Imai, Masaaki
1981   *Sixteen Ways to Avoid Saying No.* Tokyo: Nihon Keizai Shinbun.

James, William
1907   *Psychology.* New York: Holt, Rinehart & Winston.

Janney, Richard and Horst Arndt
1992   Intracultural tact versus intercultural tact. In: Richard Watts, Sachiko Ide and Konrad Ehlich (eds.), *Politeness in Language: Studies in its History, Theory and Practice,* 21-41. Berlin: Mouton de Gruyter.

Kasper, Gabriele
1984   Pragmatic comprehension in learner-native speaker discourse. *Language Learning* 34: 1-20.
1992   Pragmatic transfer. *Second Language Research* 8: 203-231.
1997   Beyond reference. In: Gabriele Kasper and Eric Kellerman (eds.), *Communication Strategies: Psycholinguistic and Sociolinguistic Perspectives*, 345-360. London: Longman.

Kasper, Gabriele and Shoshana Blum-Kulka (eds.)
1993   *Interlanguage Pragmatics.* New York: Oxford University Press.

Kasper, Gabriele and Merete Dahl
1991   Research methods in interlanguage pragmatics. *Studies in Second Language Acquisition* 13: 215-247.

Kasper, Gabriele and Eric Kellerman
1997   Introduction: Approaches to communication strategies. In: Gabriele Kasper and Eric Kellerman (eds.), *Communication Strategies: Psycholinguistic and Sociolinguistic Perspectives*, 1-13. London: Longman.

Kasper, Gabriele and Kenneth Rose
    in prep.   *Speech Act Data*. Mahwah, NJ: Lawrence Erlbaum Associates.
Kasper, Gabriele and Richard Schmidt
    1996   Developmental issues in interlanguage pragmatics. *Studies in Second Language Acquisition* 18: 149-169.
Kawate-Mierzejewska, Megumi
    1997   Back channel cues as sources for conversation breakdowns and misunderstandings. In: Jeff Johnson and Noël Houck (eds.), *Spoken Discourse Analysis*, 97-116. (Temple University Japan Working Papers in Applied Linguistics #10.) Tokyo: Temple University Japan.
Kellerman, Eric
    1979   Transfer and non-transfer: Where we are now. *Studies in Second Language Acquisition* 2: 37-57.
Kendon, Adam
    1985   Some uses of gesture. In: Deborah Tannen and Muriel Saville-Troike (eds.), *Perspectives on Silence*, 215-233. Norwood, NJ: Ablex.
    1994   Do gestures communicate? A review. *Research on Language and Social Interaction* 27: 175-200.
    1995   Gestures as illocutionary and discourse structure markers in Southern Italian conversation. *Journal of Pragmatics* 23: 247-279.
Kim, Min-Sun
    1994   Cross-cultural comparisons of the perceived importance of conversational constraints. *Human Communication Research* 21: 128-151.
Kinjo, Hiromi
    1987   Oral refusals of invitations and requests in English and Japanese. *Journal of Asian Culture* 1: 83-106.
Kita, Sotaro
    1993   Japanese adults' development of English speaking ability: Change in the language-thought process observed through spontaneous gesture. Paper presented at the Second Language Research Forum, Pittsburgh, March.
    1998   Japanese ideology of conversation and its structural manifestations: A study of *aiduchi* and head nods. Paper presented at the International Pragmatics Conference, Reims, France, July.

Kitao, Kathleen
1997   Conversational constraints and refusals in British English. *Doshisha Women's College Annual Reports of Studies* 48: 42-60.
Labov, William and David Fanshel
1977   *Therapeutic Discourse: Psychotherapy as Conversation.* New York: Academic Press.
Larsen-Freeman, Diane and Michael Long
1991   *An Introduction to Second Language Acquisition Research.* London: Longman.
Lasnik, Howard
1989   On certain substitutes for negative evidence. In: Robert J. Matthews and William Demopoulos (eds.), *Learnability and Linguistic Theory,* 89-105. Dordrecht: Kluwer.
Liao, Chao-chih
1994   *A Study on the Strategies, Maxims, and Development of Refusal in Mandarin Chinese.* Taiwan: The Crane Publishing Company.
LoCastro, Virginia
1987   Aizuchi: A Japanese conversational routine. In: Larry Smith (ed.), *Discourse across Cultures,* 101-113. New York: Prentice Hall.
Long, Michael
1980   Input, interaction and second language acquisition. Ph.D. dissertation, University of California at Los Angeles.
1981   Input, interaction, and second language acquisition. *Annals of the New York Academy of Sciences* 379, 259-278. New York.
1983a   Native speaker/non-native speaker conversation and the negotiation of comprehensible input. *Applied Linguistics* 4: 126-141.
1983b   Linguistic and conversational adjustment to non-native speakers. *Studies in Second Language Acquisition* 5: 177-193.
1996   The role of the linguistic environment in second language acquisition. In: William Ritchie and Tej Bhatia (eds.), *Handbook of Second Language Acquisition*, 413-468. San Diego: Academic Press.
in press   *Task-based Language Teaching.* Oxford: Blackwell.

Luthy, Melvin
  1983   Non-native speakers' perceptions of English 'nonlexical'
            intonation signals. *Language Learning* 3: 19-36.
Lyuh, Inook
  1992   The art of refusal: Comparison of Korean and American
            cultures. Ph.D. dissertation, Indiana University.
Mackey, Alison and Susan Gass
  1998   How do learners perceive feedback in task-based interac-
            tion? Paper presented at PacSLRF, Tokyo, March.
Maltz, Daniel and Ruth Borker
  1982   A cultural approach to male-female miscommunication.
            In: John Gumperz (ed.), *Language and Social Identity,*
            217-231. New York: Cambridge University Press.
Markee, Numa
  in prep. *Conversation Analysis.* Mahwah, NJ: Lawrence Erlbaum
            Associates.
Maynard, Senko
  1989   *Japanese Conversation.* Norwood, NJ: Ablex.
McDonough, Stephen H.
  1981   *Psychology in Foreign Language Teaching.*   London:
            George Allen and Unwin.
McNeill, David
  1966   Developmental psycholinguistics. In: Frank Smith and
            George Miller (eds.), *The Genesis of Language: A Psy-
            cholinguistic Approach,* 15-84. Cambridge, Mass: MIT
            Press.
Mehrabian, Albert
  1972   *Nonverbal Communication.* Chicago: Aldine.
Morrow, Christopher
  1995   The pragmatic effects of instruction on ESL learners' pro-
            duction of complaint and refusal speech acts. Ph.D. dis-
            sertation, State University of New York at Buffalo.
Neu, Joyce
  1990   Assessing the role of nonverbal communication in the ac-
            quisition of communicative competence in L2. In: Robin
            Scarcella, Elaine Andersen and Stephen Krashen (eds.),
            *Developing Communicative Competence in a Second Lan-
            guage,* 121-138. New York: Newbury House.
Nobuyoshi, Junko and Rod Ellis
  1993   Focused communication tasks and second language acqui-
            sition. *English Language Teaching Journal* 47: 203-210.

Patterson, Miles
    1994   Strategic functions of nonverbal exchange. In: John Daly and John Wiemann (eds.), *Strategic Interpersonal Communication*, 273-293. Hillsdale, NJ: Lawrence Erlbaum Associates.

Philp, Jenefer
    1999   Interaction, noticing and second language acquisition: An examination of learners' noticing of recasts in task-based interaction. Ph.D. dissertation, University of Tasmania.

Pica, Teresa
    1987   Second language acquisition, social interaction, and the classroom. *Applied Linguistics* 8: 3-21.
    1988   Interlanguage adjustments as an outcome of NS-NNS negotiated interaction. *Language Learning* 38: 45-73.
    1994   Research on negotiation: What does it reveal about second-language learning conditions, processes, and outcomes? *Language Learning* 44: 493-527.

Pica, Teresa and Catherine Doughty
    1985   Input and interaction in the communicative classroom: A comparison of teacher-fronted and group activities. In: Susan Gass and Carolyn Madden (eds.), *Input in Second Language Acquisition,* 115-132. Rowley, MA: Newbury House.

Pica, Teresa, Catherine Doughty and Richard Young
    1986   Making input comprehensible: Do interactional modifications help? *ITL Review of Applied Linguistics* 72: 1-25.

Pica, Teresa, Richard Young and Catherine Doughty
    1987   The impact of interaction on comprehension. *TESOL Quarterly* 21: 737-758.

Pinker, Steven
    1994   *The Language Instinct*. New York: William Morrow and Company.

Plough, India
    1994   A role for indirect negative evidence in second language acquisition. Ph.D. dissertation, Department of English, Michigan State University.
    1996   Indirect negative evidence, inductive inferencing, and second language acquisition. In: Lynn Eubank, Larry Selinker and Michael Sharwood Smith (eds.), *The Current State of Interlanguage: Studies in Honor of William E. Rutherford*, 89-105. Amsterdam: John Benjamins.

Posner, Michael
    1994   Attention: The mechanisms of consciousness. *Proceed-ings of the National Academy of Sciences* 91: 7398-7403.
Riley, Philip
    1989   'Well don't blame me': On the interpretation of pragmatic errors. In: Wieslaw Oleksy (ed.), *Contrastive Pragmatics*, 231-249. Amsterdam: John Benjamins.
Rintell, Ellen and Candace Mitchell
    1989   Studying requests and apologies: An inquiry into method. In: Shoshana Blum-Kulka, Juliane House and Gabriele Kasper (eds.), *Cross-cultural Pragmatics: Requests and Apologies,* 248-272. Norwood, NJ: Ablex.
Robinson, Mary Ann
    1992   Introspective methodology in interlanguage pragmatics research. In: Gabriele Kasper (ed.), *Pragmatics of Japanese as Native and Target Language*, 27-82. (Technical Report #3.) Manoa, HI: University of Hawai'i Press.
Rose, Kenneth
    1992   Speech acts and questionnaires: The effect of hearer response. *Journal of Pragmatics* 17: 49-62.
    1994   On the validity of discourse completion tests in non-Western contexts. *Applied Linguistics* 15: 1-14.
Rose, Kenneth and Reiko Ono
    1995   Eliciting speech act data in Japanese: The effect of questionnaire type. *Language Learning* 45: 191-223.
Rosenfeld, Harold
    1987   Conversational control functions of nonverbal behavior. In: Aron Siegman and Stanley Feldstein (eds.), *Nonverbal Behavior and Communication*, 563-601. Hillsdale, NJ: Lawrence Erlbaum Associates.
Rozelle, Richard, Daniel Druckman and James Baxter
    1997   Nonverbal behaviour as communication. In: Owen Hargie (ed.), *The Handbook of Communication Skills,* 67-102. New York: Routledge.
Rubin, Joan
    1983   How to tell when someone is saying 'no' revisited. In: Nessa Wolfson and Elliot Judd (eds.), *Sociolinguistics and Language Acquisition*, 10-17. Cambridge, MA: Newbury House.

Saleemi, Anjum
  1992   *Universal Grammar and Language Learnability.* Cam-
            bridge: Cambridge University Press.
Sasaki, Miyuki
  1998   Investigating EFL students' production of speech acts: A
            comparison of production questionnaires and role plays.
            Journal of Pragmatics 30: 457-484.
Saville-Troike, Muriel
  1989   *The Ethnography of Communication.* (2nd edition.) New
            York: Basil Blackwell.
Scarcella, Robin
  1978   Socio-drama for social interaction. *TESOL Quarterly* 12:
            41-46.
Schachter, Jacquelyn
  1988   Second language acquisition and its relationship to Uni-
            versal Grammar. *Applied Linguistics* 9: 219-235.
Schachter, Jacquelyn, Patricia Rounds, Suzanne Wright and Tamara Smith
  in press   Comparing conditions for learning syntactic patterns:
            Attentional, nonattentional, and awareness. *Applied Lin-
            guistics.*
Schegloff, Emanuel
  1982   Discourse as an interactional achievement: Some uses of
            'uh huh' and other things that come between sentences. In:
            Deborah Tannen (ed.), *Georgetown University Round Ta-
            ble on Languages and Linguistics,* 71-93. Washington,
            D.C.: Georgetown University Press.
Schmidt, Richard
  1990   The role of consciousness in second language learning.
            Applied Linguistics 11: 129-158.
  1992   Awareness and second language acquisition. *Annual Re-
            view* of *Applied Linguistics* 13: 206-226.
  1993a   Consciousness, learning and interlanguage pragmatics. In:
            Gabriele Kasper and Shoshana Blum-Kulka (eds.), *Inter-
            language Pragmatics,* 21-42. New York: Oxford Univer-
            sity Press.
  1993b   Consciousness in second language learning: Introduction.
            Paper presented at Association Internationale de Linguis-
            tique Appliquée, Amsterdam, August.
  1994   Implicit learning and the cognitive unconscious: Of artifi-
            cial grammars and SLA. In: Nick Ellis (ed.), *Implicit and*

Explicit Learning of Languages, 165-209. London: Academic Press.

Schmidt, Richard and Sylvia Nagem Frota
1986   Developing basic conversational ability in a second language: A case study of an adult learner of Portuguese. In: Richard Day (ed.), *Talking to Learn: Conversation in Second Language Acquisition*, 237-326. Rowley, MA: Newbury House.

Schwartz, Bonnie
1993   On explicit and negative data effecting and affecting competence and linguistic behavior. *Studies in Second Language Acquisition* 15: 147-163.

Seliger, Herbert
1983   The language learner as linguist: Of metaphors and realities. *Applied Linguistics* 4: 179-191.

Sheflen, Albert
1972   *Body Language and Social Order: Communication As Behavioral Control*. Englewood Cliffs, NJ: Prentice-Hall.
1973   *How Behavior Means*. Englewood Cliffs, NJ: Prentice-Hall.

Sifianou, Maria
1997   Silence and politeness. In: Adam Jaworski (ed.), *Silence: Interdisciplinary Perspectives,* 63-84. Berlin: Mouton de Gruyter.

Stern, Hans Heinrich
1983   *Fundamental Concepts of Language Teaching.* Oxford: Oxford University Press.

Swain, Merrill
1985   Communicative competence: Some roles of comprehensible input and comprehensible output in its development. In: Susan Gass and Carolyn Madden (eds.), *Input in Second Language Acquisition,* 235-253. Rowley, MA: Newbury House.
1995   Three functions of output in second language learning. In: Guy Cook and Barbara Seidlhofer (eds.), *Principle and Practice in Applied Linguistics: Studies in Honour of Henry G. Widdowson,* 125-144. Oxford: Oxford University Press.

Swain, Merrill and Sharon Lapkin
    1995   Problems in output and the cognitive processes they generate: A step towards second language learning. *Applied Linguistics* 16: 371-391.
    1998   Interaction and second language learning: Two adolescent French immersion students working together. *Modern Language Journal* 82: 320-337.

Takahashi, Tomoko and Leslie Beebe
    1987   The development of pragmatic competence by Japanese learners of English. *JALT [Japanese Association of Language Teachers] Journal* 8: 131-155.
    1993   Cross-linguistic influence in the speech act of correction. In: Gabriele Kasper and Shoshana Blum-Kulka (eds.), *Interlanguage Pragmatics,* 138-157. New York: Cambridge University Press.

Tanaka, Noriko
    1988   Politeness: Some problems for Japanese speakers of English. *JALT [Japanese Association of Language Teachers] Journal* 9: 81-102.

Tannen, Deborah
    1984   *Conversational Style: Analyzing Talk among Friends.* Norwood, NJ: Ablex.
    1985   Cross-cultural communication. In: Teun A. van Dijk (ed.), *Handbook of Discourse Analysis, Vol. 4,* 203-215. London: Academic Press.
    1990   *You Just Don't Understand.* New York: William Morrow and Company, Inc.
    1993   What's in a frame: Surface evidence for underlying expectations. In: Deborah Tannen (ed.), *Framing in Discourse,* 14-56. Oxford: Oxford University Press.

Tarone, Elaine
    1980   Communication strategies, foreigner talk, and repair in interlanguage. *Language Learning* 30: 417-431.

Thomas, Jennifer
    1983   Cross-cultural pragmatic failure. *Applied Linguistics* 4: 91-112.

Trosborg, Anna
    1995   *Interlanguage Pragmatics: Requests, Complaints, and Apologies.* Berlin. Mouton de Gruyter.

Turnbull, William
    1993   Manual for the coding of request refusals and acceptances.
                [Unpublished ms.]
    1994   An appraisal of pragmatic elicitation techniques for the
                study of social factors in language use. [Unpublished ms.]
Ueda, Keiko
    1972   Sixteen ways to avoid saying 'no' in Japan. In: John Con-
                don and Mitsuko Saito (eds.), *Intercultural Encounters
                with Japan: Communication — Contact and Conflict*, 185-
                192. Tokyo: The Simul Press.
Valian, Virginia
    1990   Logical and psychological constraints on the acquisition
                of syntax. In: Lynn Frazier and Jill de Villiers (eds.),
                Language Processing and Language Acquisition, 119-
                145. Dordrecht: Kluwer.
van Dijk, Teun
    1982   Episodes as units of discourse analysis. In: Deborah Tan-
                nen (ed.), *Analyzing Discourse: Text and Talk,* 177-195.
                Washington, D.C.: Georgetown University Press.
Varonis, Evangeline and Susan Gass
    1985a   Non-native/non-native conversations: A model for nego-
                tiation of meaning. *Applied Linguistics* 6: 71-90.
    1985b   Miscommunication in native/non-native conversation.
                Language in Society 14: 327-343.
Wagner-Gough, Judith and Evelyn Hatch
    1975   The importance of input data in second language acquisi-
                tion studies. *Language Learning* 25: 297-307.
Walters, Joel
    1980   Grammar, meaning and sociocultural appropriateness in
                second language acquisition. *Canadian Journal of Psy-
                chology* 34: 337-345.
Watanabe, Suwako
    1993   Cultural differences in framing: American and Japanese
                group discussions. In: Deborah Tannen (ed.), *Framing in
                Discourse,* 176-209. Oxford: Oxford University Press.
Watson-Gegeo, Karen
    1988   Ethnography in ESL: Defining the essentials. *TESOL
                Quarterly* 22: 575-592.
Wesche, Marjorie
    1994   Input and interaction in second language acquisition. In:
                Clare Gallaway and Brian J. Richards (eds.), *Input and*

Interaction in Language Acquisition, 219-249. Cambridge: Cambridge University Press.

White, Lydia
 1989   U*niversal Grammar and Second Language Acquisition.* Amsterdam: John Benjamins.

White, Sheida
 1989   A study of Americans and Japanese. *Language in Society* 18: 59-76.

Wolfson, Nessa
 1981   Compliments in cross-cultural perspective. *TESOL Quarterly* 15: 117-124.
 1989   *Perspectives: Sociolinguistics and TESOL.* New York: Newbury House.

Wolfson, Nessa, Thomas Marmor and Steve Jones
 1989   Problems in the comparison of speech acts across cultures. In: Shoshana Blum-Kulka, Juliane House and Gabriele Kasper (eds.), *Cross-cultural Pragmatics: Requests and Apologies,* 174-196. Norwood, NJ: Ablex.

Yamashita, Sayoko
 1996   *Six Measures of JSL Pragmatics.* (Technical Report #14.) Manoa, HI: University of Hawai'i Press.

Yngve, Victor
 1970   On getting a word in edgewise. *Chicago Linguistic Society* 6: 567-578.

Yule, George
 1997   *Referential Communication Tasks.* Mahwah, NJ: Lawrence Erlbaum Associates.

Yule, George and Elaine Tarone
 1997   Investigating communication strategies in L2 reference: Pros and cons. In: Gabriele Kasper and Eric Kellerman (eds.), *Communication Strategies: Psycholinguistic and Sociolinguistic Perspectives*, 17-30. London: Longman.

Subject index

Author index

Andersen, Roger 153
Archibald, John 186
Ard, Josh 153
Arndt, Horst 135, 138
Aston, Guy 138, 144
Austin, John L. 105

Bachman, Lyle 131
Bardovi-Harlig, Kathleen 14, 16-17, 24, 25, 31-32, 37, 39, 41, 51, 52, 66, 147, 153, 167, 183, 195-196, 196-197, 198, 201, 202, 217, 219, 220
Baxter, James 109
Beebe, Leslie 12-14, 15-16, 17, 18, 24, 30-31, 35, 37, 38, 39, 41, 66, 67, 68, 69, 70, 111-112, 149, 158, 164, 165, 217, 218, 219
Bialystok, Ellen 132-133
Birdsong, David 188
Bley-Vroman, Robert 159
Bloomfield, Leonard 186
Blum-Kulka, Shoshana 1, 10, 13, 37, 132, 158, 194-195, 199-200
Borker, Ruth 221
Brown, James D. 33

Canale, Michael 131
Cazden, Courtney 187
Celce-Murcia, Marianne 131
Chaudron, Craig 21
Chen, Xing 2, 17
Chomsky, Noam 183, 197
Clancy, Patricia 85-86, 88, 220

Cohen, Andrew 23, 217
Cook, Vivian 181, 183
Corder, S. Pit 132
Cummings, Martha 12, 30-31, 37

Dahl, Merete 25, 29, 30, 132
Detmer, Emily 33
Dörnyei, Zoltan 131, 202
Doughty, Catherine 176, 177
Druckman, Daniel 109
Duff, Patsy 21
Duncan, Starkey 84, 87, 220

Edmondson, Willis 4, 34-35, 83, 84, 87, 88, 108, 137-138, 219, 223
Ekman, Paul 109, 110-111, 222
Ellis, Rod 131, 132, 159, 198
Erickson, Frederick 81, 82

Færch, Claus 22, 132, 133, 136
Fanshel, David 5-7, 41, 67, 68, 165, 167
Fiksdal, Susan 24, 82, 138
Friesen, Wallace 109, 222
Frota, Sylvia Nagem 198

Gass, Susan 9, 14, 21, 22, 23, 24-25, 132, 146, 153, 155, 158, 159, 160, 171, 174-175, 176, 177, 179, 186, 188, 189, 191, 193, 194, 198, 225
Goffman, Erving 30

Studies on Language Acquisition

Edited by Peter Jordens

Mouton de Gruyter · Berlin · New York